WHEN CULTURE MEETS ARCHITECTURE

DESIGN MEDIA PUBLISHING LIMITED

Contents

4   New Cultural Centre in Madrid

10   South Miami Dade Cultural Centre

18   ASSEMBLING – Associative Cultural Centre

22   Ordup Culture Building

28   The Montarville – Boucher la Bruère Public Library

34   Gijon Aquarium

40   Human Evolution Museum

46   Fjord Museum

50   New Cultural Centre in Ranica

54   New Centre of Lehen

60   Gabriela Mistral Cultural Centre

66   Sjakket

74   Cultural Centre Miguel Delibes

80   Docks of Paris

86   Zhongguancun Cultural Centre

90   Regional Cultural Centre Letterkenny

94   Cultural Centre Bafile

98   New Jiangwan Culture Centre

104 Rio Salado Audubon Centre

110 Norveg Coast Cultural Centre

116 Maritime Centre Vellamo

122 Library and Media Centre for the University of Guadalajara

128 Jacob and Wilhelm Grimm Centre

134 Ann Arbor District Library – Traverwood Branch

138 Beth Sholom

146 Kupferberg Holocaust Resource Centre and Archives

152 Peres Centre for Peace

158 Danfoss Universe

162 Olympic House and Park

170 Mora River Aquarium

176 Aquarium Of San Sebastian

182 Ibaiondo Civic Centre

188 Documentation and Information Centre of Bergen-Belsen Memorial

192 EDF Archives Centre

196 Ars Electronica Centre

202 Nanjing University Performing Arts Centre

208 New Art Exchange

214 Prism Contemporary Art/Plastic Sensations

218 The Brother Stephen Debourg Performing Arts Centre

222 Verkatehdas Arts and Congress Centre

230 Peppermint Bay

236 Art Gallery of Alberta

242 De Hangar, Eindhoven

246 Cultuurfabriek

250 Messel Pit Visitor Information Centre

258 Provintial Mediatheque Ugo Casiraghi

264 Art and Culture Centre Cool

270 Index

New Cultural Centre in Madrid

Location: Madrid, Spain **Designed by:** FÜNDC (C. GARCIA & P. MARTIN, Architects) **Completion date:** 2011 **Photos©:** FÜNDC **Site area:** 10,280 square metres

The project has a couple of unprecedented design solutions such as "mega-tree-pots" and a transformable hall. The pots allow for the growth of medium-large trees above an underground parking, making possible green areas where usually just hard squares are found. The hall allows for an use modification on the cultural building programme, as it can switch between exhibition promenade and auditorium mode through the manipulation of movable floor decks.

The built size of the intervention, both under and above ground comes near to 20,000 square metres. It consists on the urbanisation through a new uninterrupted stone pavement, fountains and "mega-tree-pots" around a New Cultural Centre building. The latter is composed of two different architectural typologies, old and new, which work on a symbiotic manner providing traditional and transformable spaces. Under these areas and building a double-deck parking absorbs the vehicle impact working together with underground roads and bus stops, freeing the upper square spaces to pedestrians and bikes.

"This intervention changes the traditional way of understanding new pedestrian areas on built environment as it does not choose between pedestrians or cars but accepts both, re-positioning them." as explained by architect Cesar Garcia. "No need for road restrictions when you can reposition them underground. No need for lack of parking places as you can multiply them on levels. No need for flat hard public squares when you can grow large trees, necessary for urban comfort on this climate."

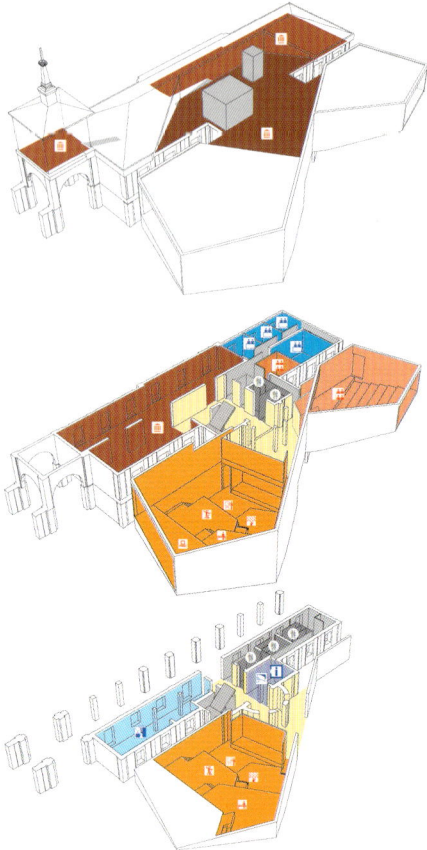

1. Front plaza
2. Side view of the entrance
3. Front façade
4. Side view of façade

3

4

1. Building with plaza in the night

1. Building with plaza in the night
2. Night view
3. Foyer

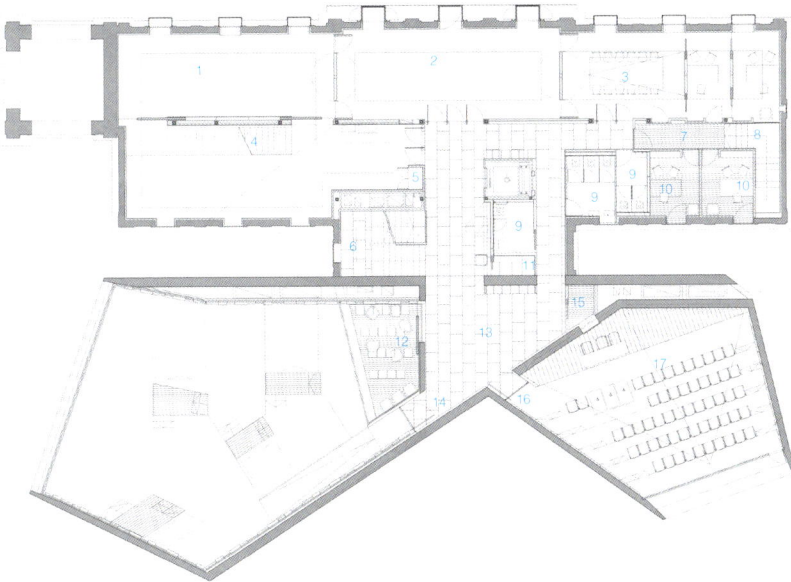

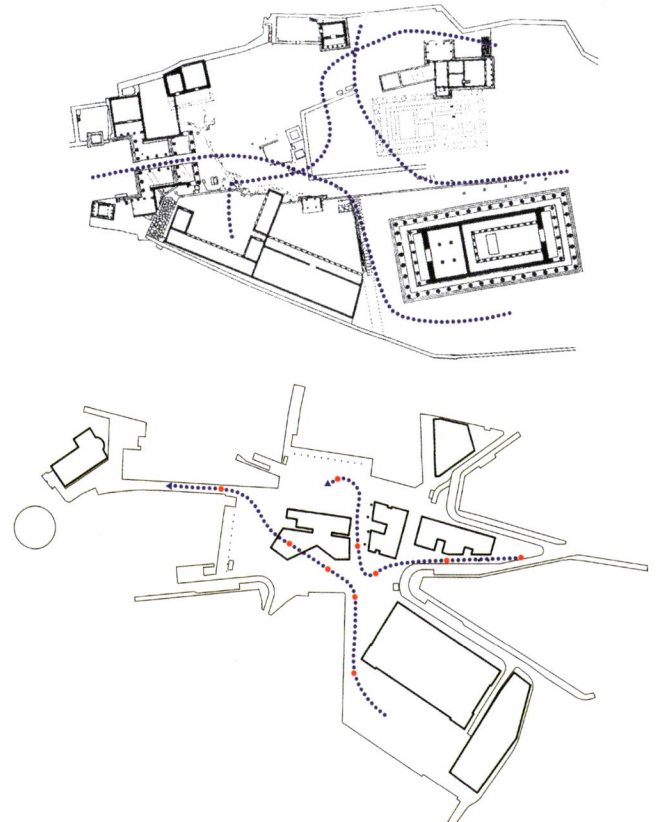

3

1. Exhibition hall
2. Exhibition hall
3. Expo / offices / meeting
4. Tower ladder
5. Cabinet
6. Stairway to terrace
7. Access hall offices
8. PB ladder
9. Toilet
10. Office
11. Wardrobe
12. Coffee / standby
13. Hall
14. Multifunctional hall access
15. Room support
16. Multifunctional hall access
17. Room

1. Special-designed stair and resting area
2. Exhibition space / hall
3. Lecture room seating detail

South Miami Dade Cultural Centre

Location: Florida, USA **Designed by:** Arquitectonica **Completion date:** 2009 **Photos©:** Robin Hill **Area:** 6,643 square metres

The facility consists of a 6,643-square-metres cultural arts centre that includes a 3,158-square-metres stage-house with 1,579-square-metres front-of-house and public lobby space. The centre is a 966-seat facility that is intended to be used as a multi-purpose community centre to stage theatre and orchestral productions as well as local functions such as graduations and school plays.

The back-of-house consists primarily of staff accommodations, building services, administrative offices as well as receiving and storage facilities. The activity building comprises a 700-square-metre structure with high ceilings for the gallery, dance rehearsal and classroom spaces. It is intended that these can be used for local community meetings and after-hours adult education classes.

The two buildings are joined by an outdoor promenade leading to a gently sloping lawn for outdoor concerts and festivals along the Black Creek Canal. Outdoor activities along the canal edge aid in the activation of the waterfront in tandem with the Park and Recreation.

The design for this new cultural arts and community centre is based on movement. The buildings reflect the spirit of movement, moving the patron through a visual as well as physical experience, making the patron a performer. The flow of people begins with the monumental ramps at the exterior of the building and continues through to the brushed aluminum grand-stair that delivers each person to the orchestra level and balcony levels above. Glimpses of people circulating behind a panelite-screened wall punctured with openings of various sizes at all the balcony levels, reinforces the idea that the building is designed with two prosceniums. The obvious proscenium is the one located within the performance hall as the traditional stage is set; the exterior frame around the full height curtain wall forms the second, subtler proscenium.

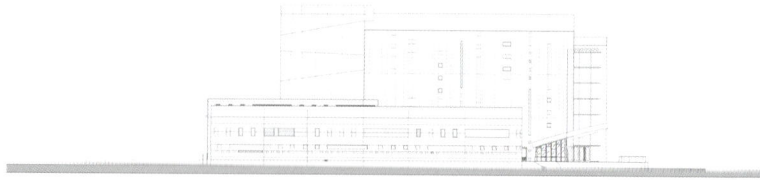

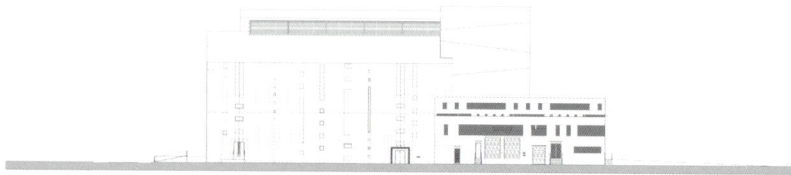

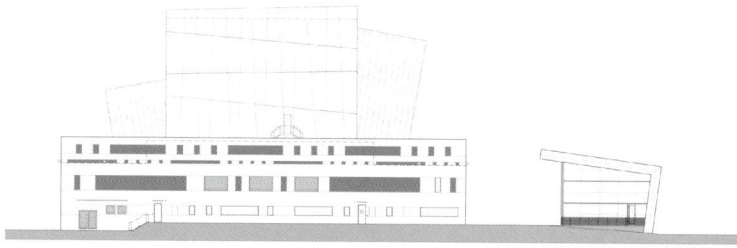

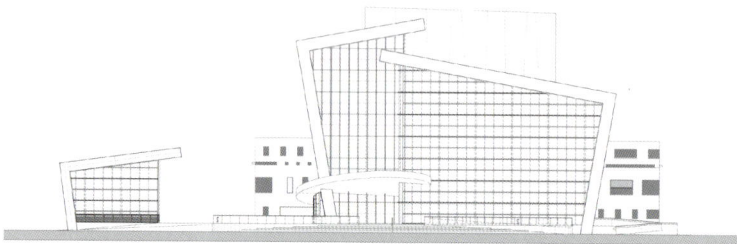

1. Overall building viewed from lawn
2. Front façade in dusk

1. Front façade at night
2. Entrance lobby

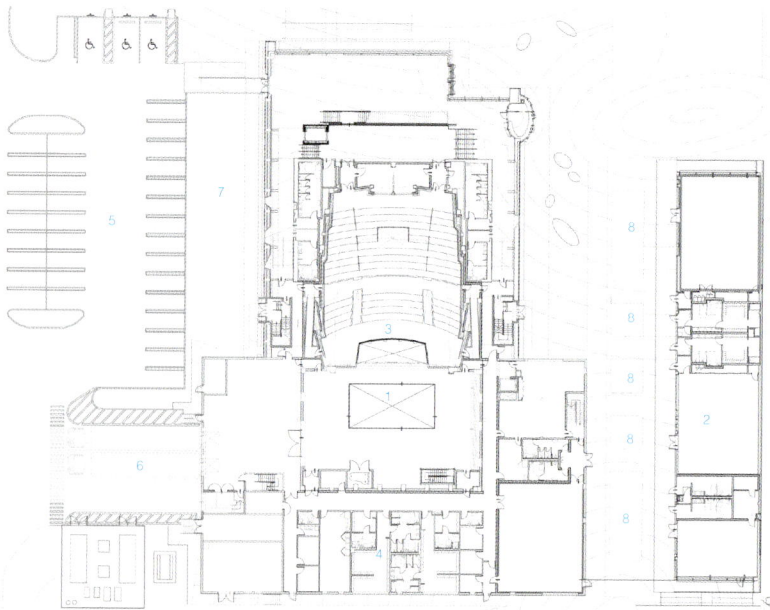

1. Main building
2. Activity building
3. Theatre
4. Dressing rooms
5. Parking
6. Loading area
7. Lawn
8. Planter

1

2

1. Office
2. Dressing room
3, 4. Rehearsal hall

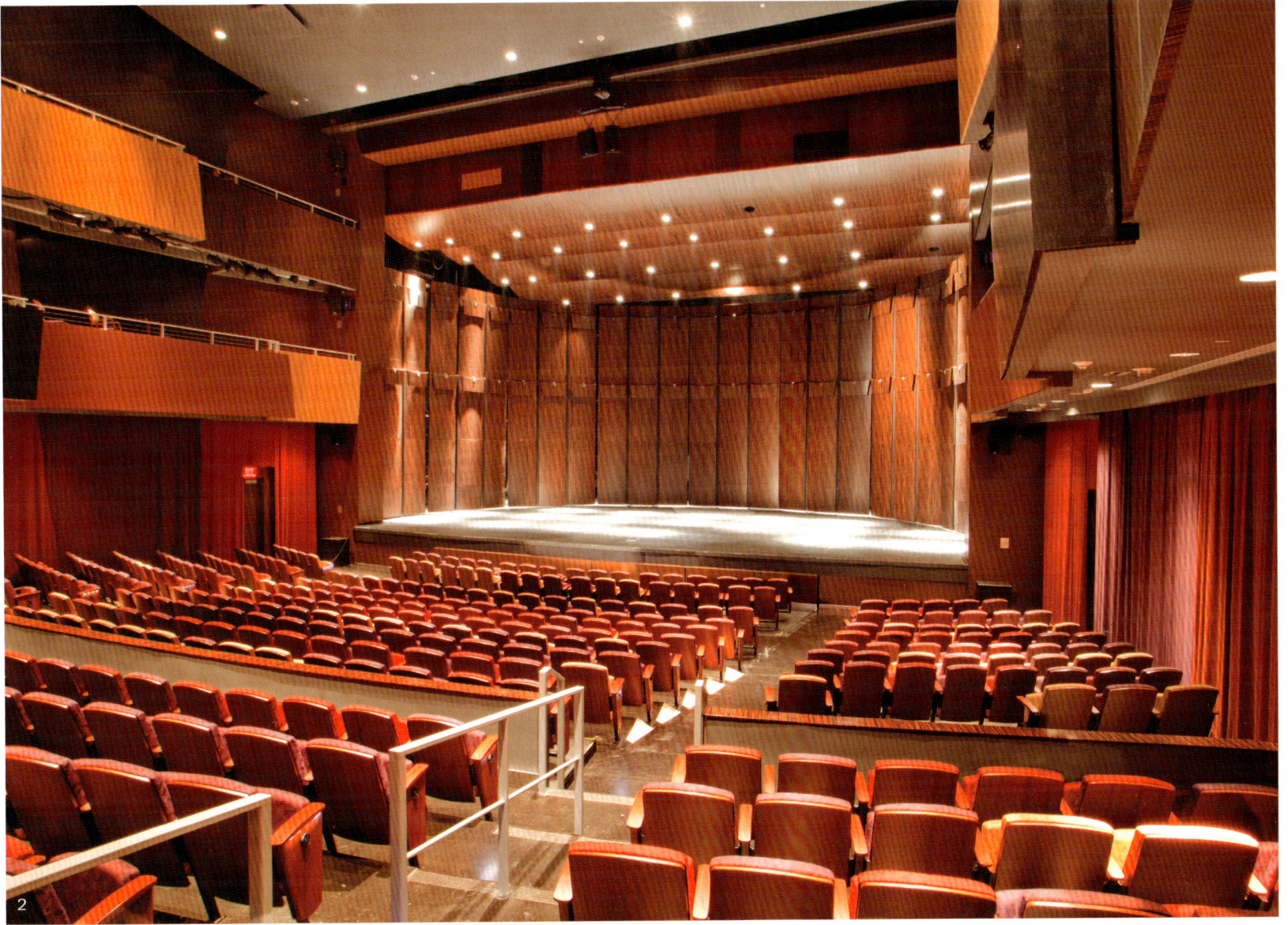

1-3. Auditorium

ASSEMBLING – Associative Cultural Centre

Location: Saint-Germain-Lès-Corbeil, France **Designed by:** RMDM Architects **Completion date:** 2009
Photos©: Hervé Abbadie **Building area:** 2,450 square metres

The amazing building of Associative Cultural Centre, which is located near Paris, France is designed by RMDM Architects. True and creative, RMDM Architects agency puts its energy in the research of a sensuous architecture, responding to the events that surround it, entire and poetical, ambitious indeed, but far from the obviousness of the conventional.

This is a modern cultural building design composed of two entities: a library (rehabilitation) and a multi-activities hall (construction) linked by a shared lobby and courtyard garden. The project is built around the reception spaces and a garden under control. The garden itself can structure the space, like a cloister where the spaces and functions eventually meet.

This diversity programme serves in an architectural design, where a game of simple and readable volumes, each incorporating a functional cluster. The concrete structure is made distinctive by the process of materials: the exterior is clad with horizontal strips of poplar wood and ceramic tiles.

The linear frontage device is important. Indeed in order to minimise the visual impact from surrounding houses, the project extends as much as possible. It is a project sculpted by its programme, with its volume obviously becoming more complex in its division. Developing its own identity, this comfortable cultural building is subtly inserted in its environment.

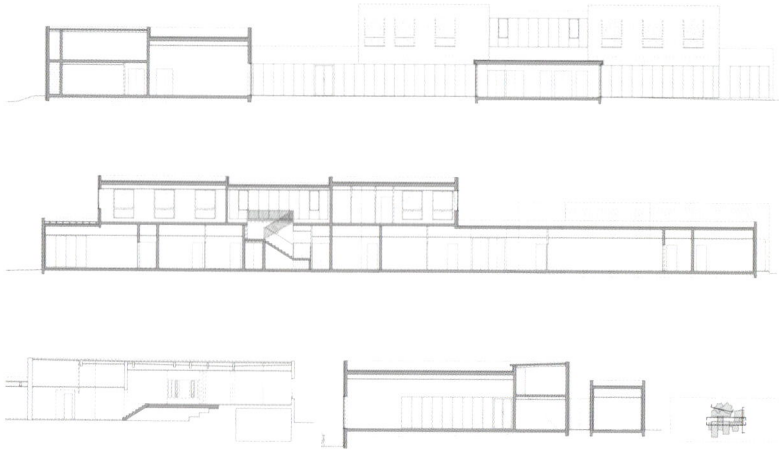

1. South façade
2. West façade, the place
3. West façade, the square

1, 2. Patio, the garden
3. Interior gallery

1 Library/rehabilitation
2 Multi-activities centre/construction

Ordup Culture Building

Location: Ordup, Denmark **Designed by:** Søren Robert Lund Arkitekter and Studio NORD **Completion date:** 2008 **Photos©:** Søren Robert Lunbd arkitekter **Construction area:** 3,500 square metres

Ordup Culture Building is a compact hybrid building with emphasis not only on design but also on the content.

It is developed in a user-driven design process where a library, sports facilities, auditorium and teaching are weaved into one consistent building. The green iconographic envelope is embracing these programmes in one gesture allowing the difference of each component to become one.

The idea about an outer and inner compression/deformity is underlined in the choice of materials, where the outer shape is defined by a green glass fiber coated façade, which opens up like a portal to the inner deformity. In the interior, the border between the different functions, are a mix between concrete surfaces and open glass areas. These compressions and deformation motif are used on the vertical surfaces and in the horizontal organisation of the building and is recognisable as two different elements weaved together.

On the ground level all floors are green as a carpet of artificial grass. On the first floor the grass and by that the nature, is pulled up by the green slopes and creating a bridge throughout the building from east to west.

As a central crossing point in the building the main stair and the assist stair are placed as an element that both express the vertical deformity of the figure, but also uses the horizontal surfaces in the building. The stair is designed like a sculpture steel element and this gives the motif to the rest of the building surfaces covered with steel.

The iconographic character of the design allows for a renegotiation of the typology of the cultural building. It neither expresses the dryness and dullness of the library nor the rigidity of the sports building. The envelopes iconographic nature instead becomes a openness of interpretation, a building that will grow with its use. It becomes a building that reinterprets the historian Greek gymnasium where body and soul were given equal weight.

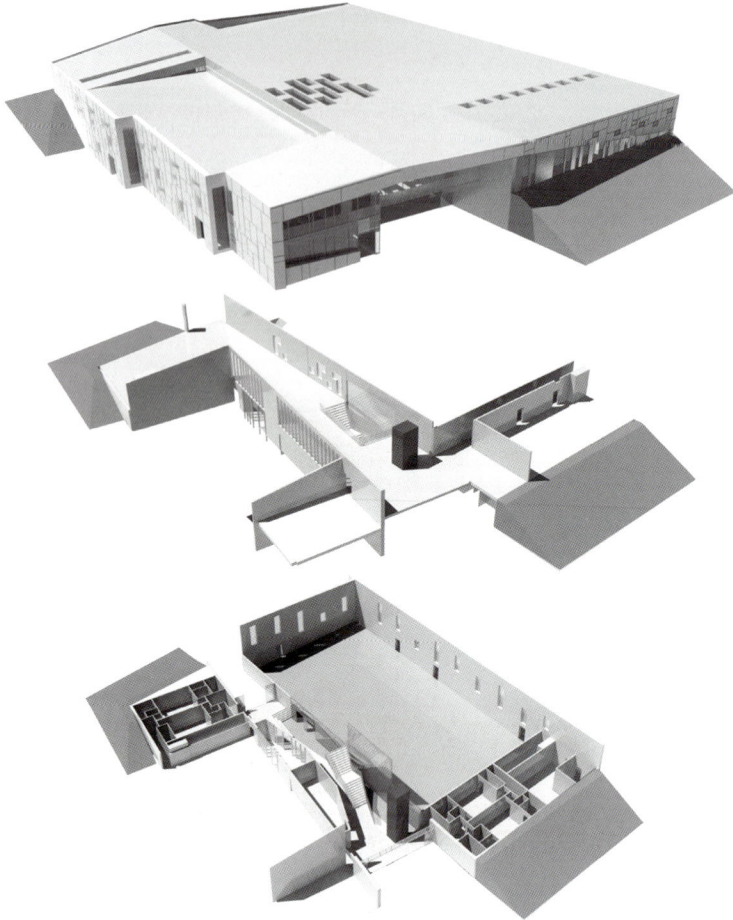

1. Façade detail
2. Multipurpose hall façade towards the park
3. East façade
4. Façade detail

3

4

1

2

1. Multipurpose hall
2. Lobby
3. Flexible sports facility
4. Stairs

3

4

1. Entrance
2. Hall
3. Reception
4. Gym
5. Library

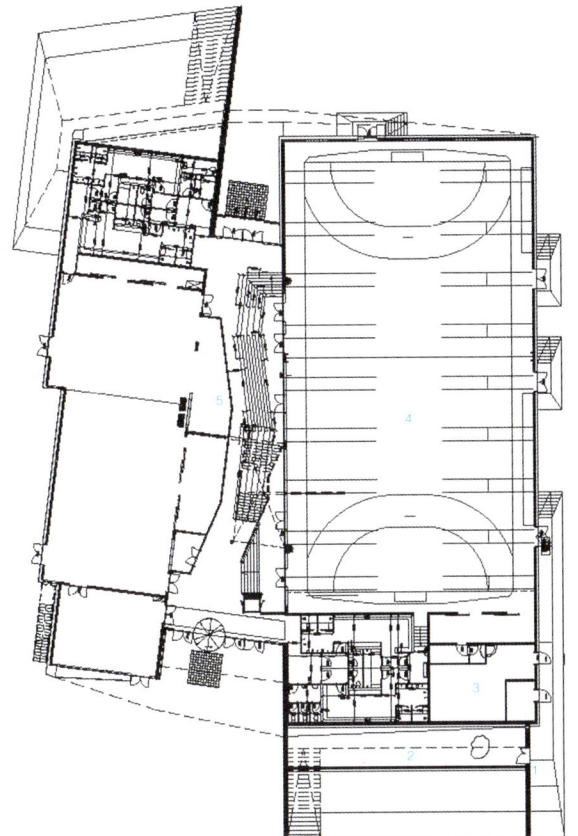

1

1-3. Exhibition hall

2

3

The Montarville – Boucher la Bruère Public Library

Location: Montreal, Canada **Designed by:** Brière, Gilbert + Associés, Architecture & Design Urbain
Completion: 2009 **Photos©:** Christian Perreault

This project includes an atrium, a new entrance hall, a new library promenade, a new loans counter and a complete reorganisation of all the library collections. After an initial assessment of the library's current context, it was the untapped potential for a visceral connection to the wooded area in the adjoining Rivière aux Pins Park that was the stimulus for the conceptual approach and further development of that idea.

Inspired by the formal logic of the existing building (four similar squares that revolve around a central core), the expansion suggests for one of these squares a shift in emphasis and an opening up to the nearby woods. This establishes new, open-ended connections between the building and its surrounding environment, redefining the heart of the library and ensuring a comprehensive unity, integrating the existing building with both the new addition and the adjacent woods.

In that sense, the two main elements that give structure to the landscape and clarify its harmonious integration are a large wooded area completely open to nature and a new library promenade, a formal exterior pathway that runs through the entire site.

The woods are an identifying element visible from the street and the surrounding area, heralding the presence of a cultural institution in an urban landscape. The three floors of the new extension mean lower costs and preserve as much as possible the trees adjacent to the building. The three storeys are home to the library's three general collections – books for children, adolescents and adults.

Taking advantage of the natural topography of the site and of the proximity of the trees, a large three-storey glass wall allows for diverse visual links between the indoor spaces and the woods. Consequently, each clientele (children, adolescents, adults and senior citizens) benefits from a distinct relationship with the vegetation, the trees and the foliage, which inspire calm, silence and rejuvenation.

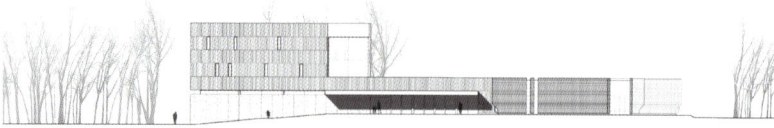

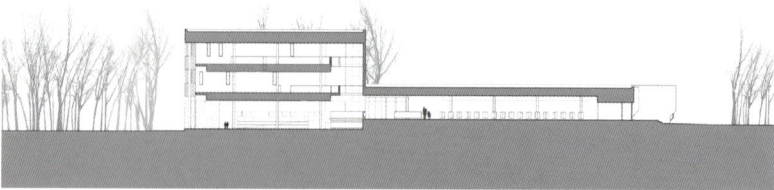

1. Overall building viewed from lawn
2. Side view of the building
3. Main entrance

1. Back façade
2. Library

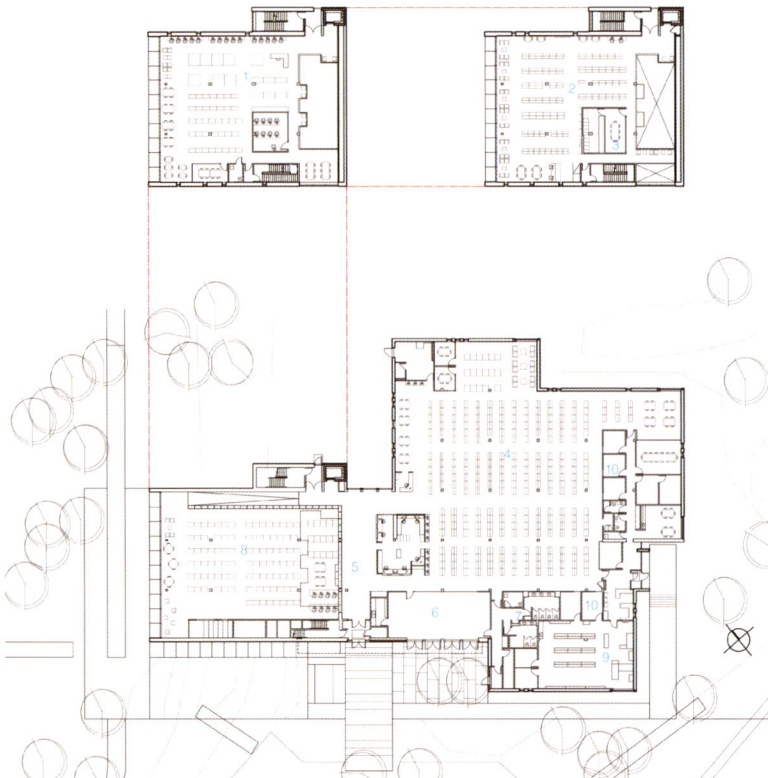

1. Audiovisual
2. References and e-library
3. Heritage hall
4. Documentary room
5. Hall
6. Multipurpose room
7. Toilets
8. Youth sector
9. Service technique
10. Professional offices

2

1 Interior access detail
2. Entrance of the library

Gijon Aquarium

Location: Gijon, Spain **Designed by:** Alvaro Planchuelo **Completion date:** 2007 **Photos©:** Studio Alvaro Planchuelo, Ricardo Santonja, Alberto Cubas **Area:** 4,650 square metres

The Gijon Aquarium is located at the end of the urban renewal for Poniente beach recuperation, the seashore façade of the city during the 20th century. The proposed solarium was formerly occupied by boat construction companies, today abandoned and demolished, leaving behind just the docks for ship construction.

The aquarium pretends to integrate itself with its surroundings using these docks to creating a slightly curved façade toward a great entrance plaza, which closes the beach areas and the west seaside walk to the remaining industrial zones left in the bay.

Externally symbolic models are used based in the main feature of the city of Gijon: its vocation port. The volume setting refers to its tradition: wood and steel boxes stacked in the port arrived from world's oceans and seas.

The interior offers an ambitious collection. A virtual tour starting and finishing in the port of Gijon, offers the major wildlife sanctuaries underwater we know. It goes from the river Cantabrian coast, the Atlantic, Caribbean Sea, the cold waters... to the tropics, the Red Sea, Indian Ocean, the subtropical waters, etc. The themed environments, the soft light and the colours, accompany visitors on their journey. Each aquarium claims to be a world in itself, a recreation of each ecosystem, a living witness box of distant worlds.

The building is divided into two main volumetric zones, the fluvial aquarium, located in the sea over the dock, and the oceans aquarium or land building. A ground floor hall, located between the two volumes, gives access to complementary placements: shop, screening room, workshop for teaching, offices, restaurant and dock recovery of marine mammals. The volumetric configuration references the port tradition of the city; using prismatic masses, wooden stacking between stainless steel elements.

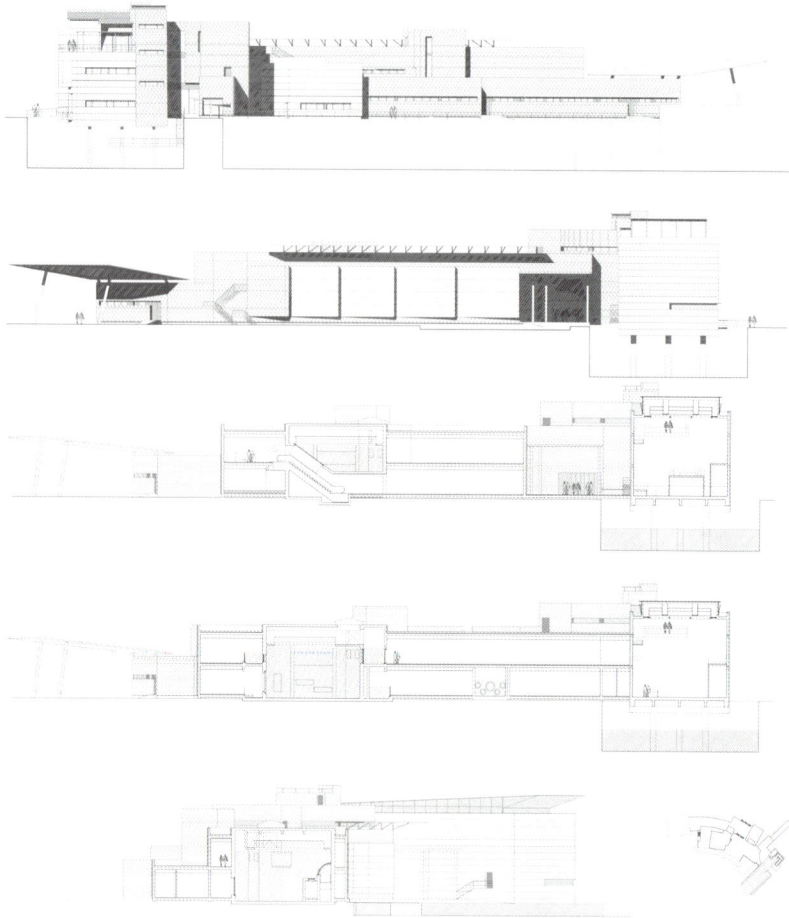

1. Aerial view
2. Back façade
3. Overall view of the building

2

3

1. Façade viewed across water
2. Canopy
3. Side view of façade

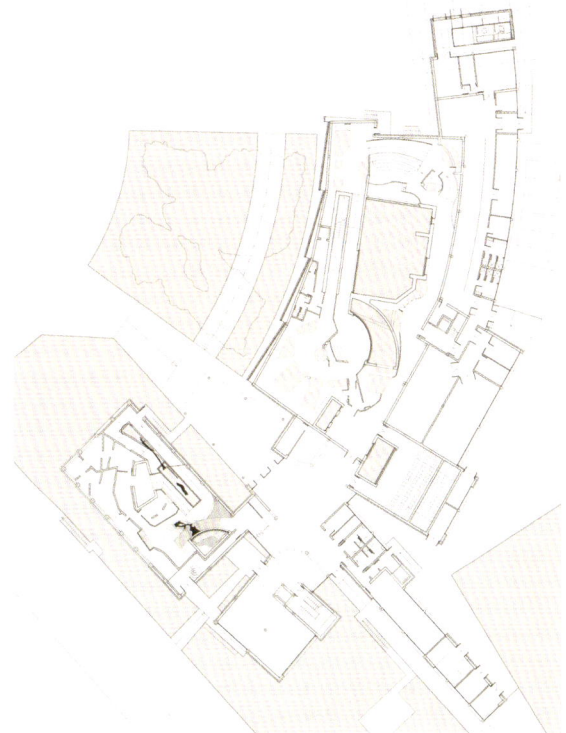

Ground floor plan

1, 3. Interior landscape
2. Interior bridge

Site plan

Human Evolution Museum

Location: Burgos, Spain **Designed by:** Juan Navarro Baldeweg **Completion date:** 2009 **Photos©:** Courtesy of Juan Navarro Baldeweg; Val Vázquez Sequeiros **Area:** 8,746 square metres

The project consists of a cluster of three-dimensional pieces – Museum of Human Evolution, Human Evolution Research Centre, Congress Centre and Auditorium – grouped into a compact unitary volume. The museum occupies a central position in the building and also in the project's origin, setting the goals in the overall building organisation.

Metaphorically speaking, the pieces are: a basket, some boxes, and a cape that covers these objects. Two of the boxes are dark and closed, one is open on one side, the last one is a transparent box. The basket envelops the museum. The dark boxes are the conference halls (large and small), the transparent box is an exhibition hall (for all sorts of objects) and the semi-open box is the research centre. The whole ensemble is covered by a flexible, waving sheet that shelters the various pieces.

The museum interior is a large area with abundant top lighting. It houses the prisms or sections of earth that suggest fragments of the landscape at the nearby Atapuerca site. It is easy to imagine this environment as a greenhouse in which the subsoil also takes on great visual importance. The corridors or "gorges" boxed in between the prisms are used for educational presentations of the geological or paleontological aspects of the archaeological site. From these corridors one can appreciate the strata that define and contextualise the deposits of human and animal bones and the remains of their technology in the evolutionary process. What they explain is expressed using architectural resources: the walls hold the information and at the same lime recreate the spatial experience of the excavation profiles and the strata of the land.

All the rear of these large prisms trays or areas are set aside for a more conventional part of the museum, for objects and installations on three floors. These floors are linked by ramps that permit cross-views of them and, hence their exhibition areas, with the possibility of integrating their contents.

The building structure is both concrete and mixed concrete – steel. The siding material is a double screen system that combines transparent and silver glass opaque glazed surfaces, steel panels and amber stone. The roof is also aluminium and glass.

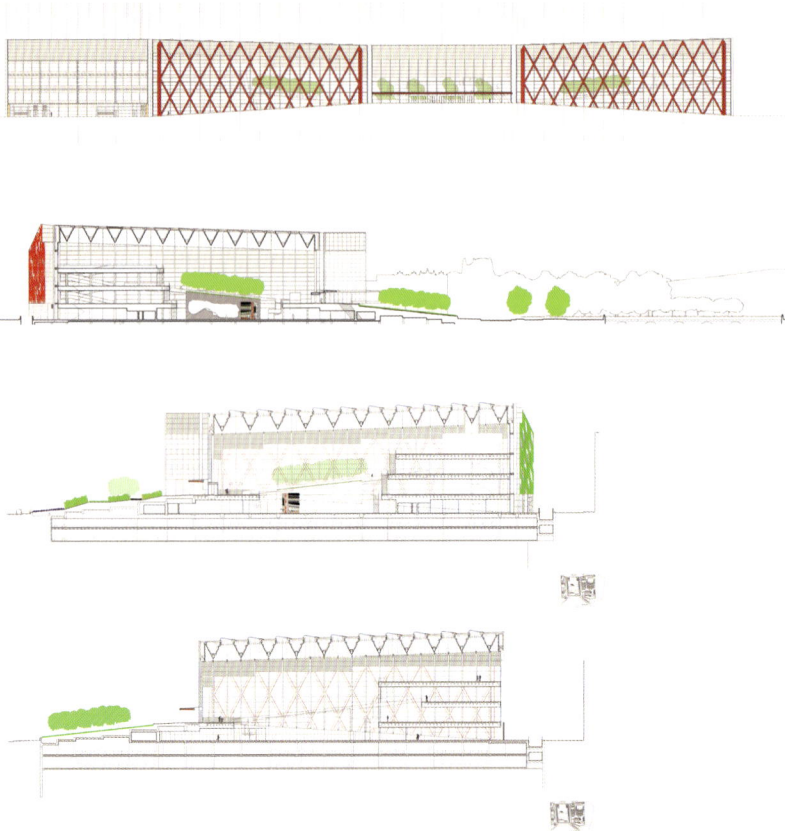

1. Aerial view
2. Main entrance

2

1. Façade detail
2. Building surrounded by greenery

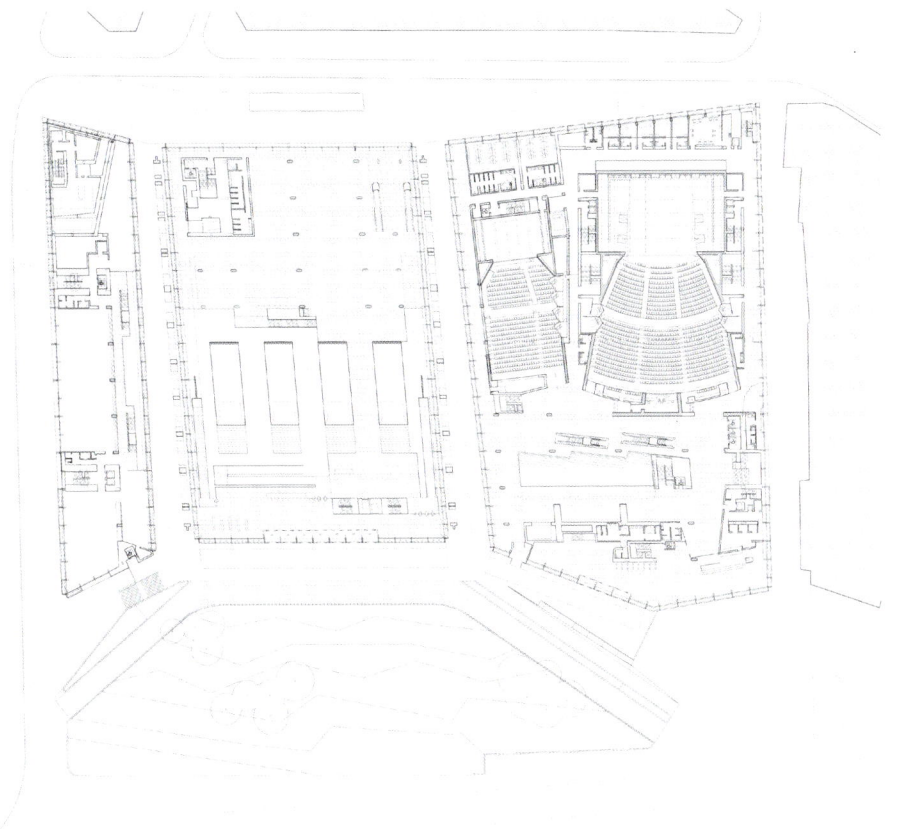

Ground floor plan

1. Canopy
2. Façade detail
3. Interior landscape

3

Fjord Museum

Location: Québec, Canada **Designed by:** Menkès Shooner Dagenais LeTourneux Architectes/Dupuis LeTourneux Architectes in consortium with BCS + M Architectes **Completion date:** 2004 **Photos©:** Steve Montpetit

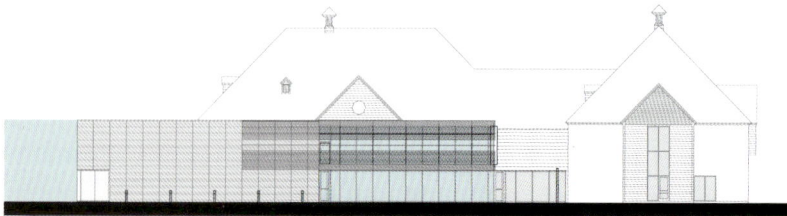

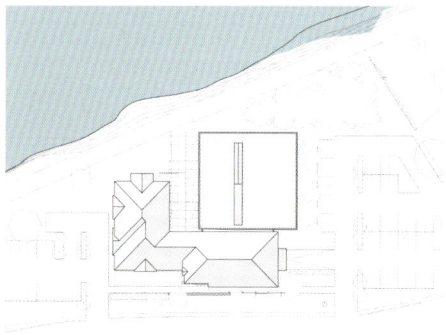

Along the north shore of the St. Lawrence and stretching deep into the rugged Saguenay Fjord, the landscape leaves an indelible and inescapable sense of existing on the edge. That edge is marked as a sharply etched line between land and water, between an almost impenetrable wilderness and an ancient but unpredictable base for communication, commerce and transport.

Along the river, wide valleys etched out by powerful ice flows millions of years ago sweep down from the north but remain above sea level and have provided a viable if sometimes precarious agricultural livelihood for its European settlers. In contrast, the Saguenay Fjord was scoured long and deep leaving an awesome shoreline that is dramatic, raw and often uninhabitable. At the same time, its mix of salt and fresh water and the relative shallowness of its entry into the St. Lawrence have ensured a rich aquatic life below its grey-blue surface.

The modest Fjord Mueseum rests on the shores of Baie des Ha! Ha! In the hamlet of La Baie 222 kilometres northeast of Quebec City. This village-owned interpretive facility is intended to celebrate as well as explain this unique biodiversity and the social and cultural history it has helped support. A simple but elegantly detailed box that conceals some difficult functional solutions, the $3.3-million expansion plays transparency against opacity and in doing so, introduces a subversive twist to local convention.

It was there that an abstracted "billboard," played out against the church, and based on an interpretation of traditional eel nets stretching along the local tidal flats, introduced their fascination with the idea of mediating architectural screens. Their use, LeTourneux explains, is about "the whole idea of openness and protection while at the same time you get to see something but you see it through the filter of architecture."

1, 2. Façade detail
3. Terrace

1. Side view of the building
2. Reception
3. Entrance seen from the lobby

3

Ground floor plan - Museum
1. Main entrance hall
2. Multimedia room
3. Didactical exhibition
4. Permanent exhibition
5. Temporary exhibition
6. Reception and preparation room
7. Collections
Ground floor plan – Community Centre
8. Multipurpose room
9. Hall
10. Office
11. Classroom
12. Studio

The first floor plan – Museum
1. Hall
2. Offices
3. Collections
4. Meeting room
5. Storage
6. Projection room
7. Observation footbridge
The first floor plan – Community Centre
8. Hall
9. Office
10. Domremy room
11. Filles d'Isabelle room
12. Dance studio

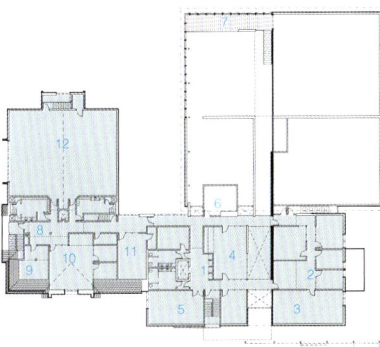

New Cultural Centre in Ranica

Location: Ranica, Italy **Designed by:** DAP studio/Elena Sacco – paolo danelli; arch. Paola Giaconia
Completion date: 2010 **Photos©:** Alessandra Bello **Construction area:** Public library: 850 sqm,
Kindergarten: 370 sqm, Auditorium: 230 sqm, Dance and Theatre School: 310 sqm, Bar: 50 sqm
Award: OAB Award 2011

The city of Ranica, in the province of Bergamo, Italy, inaugurated its new Cultural Centre. The project, designed by DAP studio and Paola Giaconia, is the outcome of a competition launched by the Municipality of Ranica in 2005 to endow the town with an important institution that would augment its cultural and social life.

The recently opened cultural centre was completed in less than two years of construction, and represents a new cultural and urbanistic beacon in the territory, laying the foundations for an alternative urban organisation. Thanks to this new building, the medieval town is able to revitalise its historical urban fabric by fastening it to a new contemporary hub, capable of nourishing the surrounding territory. In its devotion to culture and cultural enrichment, the institution plays a fundamental role in defining the spaces for the community. "The Cultural Centre is conceived as a new catalyst of urban life. Not only is the building a laboratory for education and information, but it also becomes a new "piazza" where people can meet and where citizens can reinforce their sense of belonging to their territory," the architects explain.

The building – housing a public library, an auditorium, a kindergarten, and a school for dance and theatre – is made of two volumes, one laid on the top of the other, centring on an interior courtyard capturing natural light and attracting pedestrians. The building hosts a new "piazza", a new meeting point for the citizens. In this sense, the project for the new Cultural Centre reconceives the ground. The building maintains harmony with the surrounding landscape. The lower volume is transparent, revealing the activities, which take place inside to passerby, stirring their curiosity. The upper volume sits on its top and becomes an urban signal. Its translucent polycarbonate sheets glow with vibrant tints and allow the silhouettes of people to be seen through the colourful watery façade.

The snow-white and sober interiors reveal a complexity, which endows the spaces and the activities taking place in them with a powerful dynamism. In the vast double-height space of the library the various functional areas appear as independent volumes, connected by means of elevated catwalks and visually linked to the central patio. The interior spaces become a representation of a lively urban scene where the various places are connected by a grid of paths, to be walked through as well as enjoyed in moments of pause and encounter.

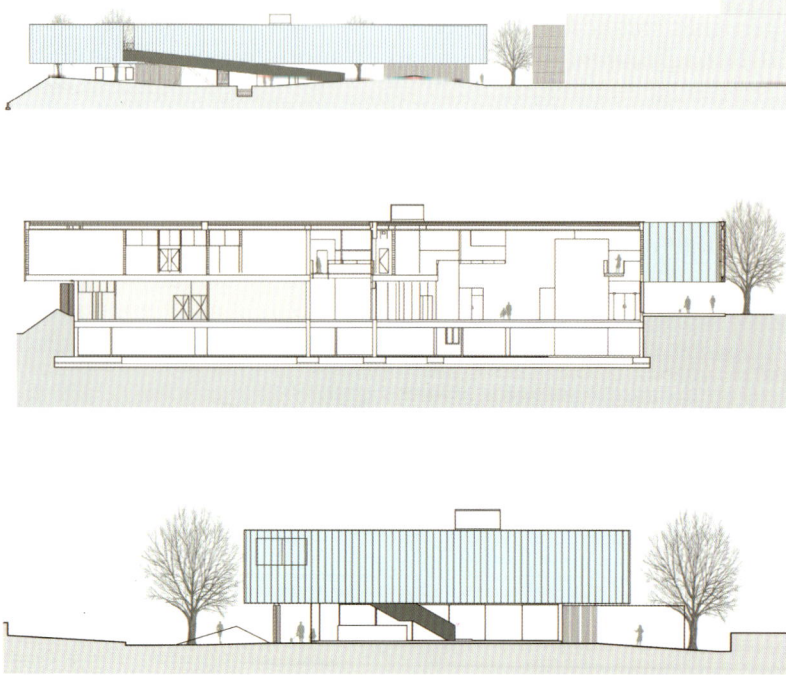

1. The interior courtyard capturing natural light and attracting pedestrians
2. Side view of colourful watery façade
3. Main façade view
4. The Cultural Centre stirs the urban landscape aesthetically and winks at the silvery shimmers of the nearby mountains

3

4

1. View from the top of the reception
2. Transparent entrance
3, 4. The library

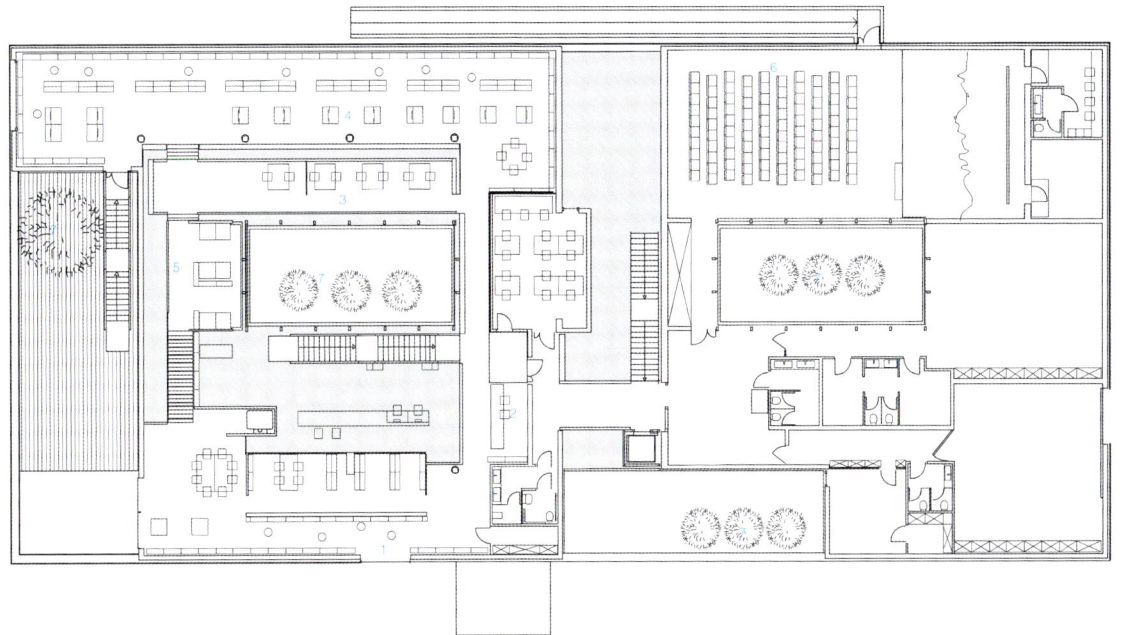

1. Entrance
2. Reception
3. Staff office
4. Library
5. Café
6. Auditorium
7. Courtyard

New Centre of Lehen

Location: Salzburg, Austria **Designed by:** Architekturbüro HALLE 1 **Completion date:** 2009 **Photos©:** Angelo Kaunat (Salzburg), Mag. Gebhard Sengmüller (Wiem) **Construction area:** 12,023 sqm **Awards:** Otto Wgner Städtebaupreis "Raum:Werk:Lehen", 2007/Anerkennung Landesarchitekturpreis Salzburg, 2008/2009 European Steel Design Award

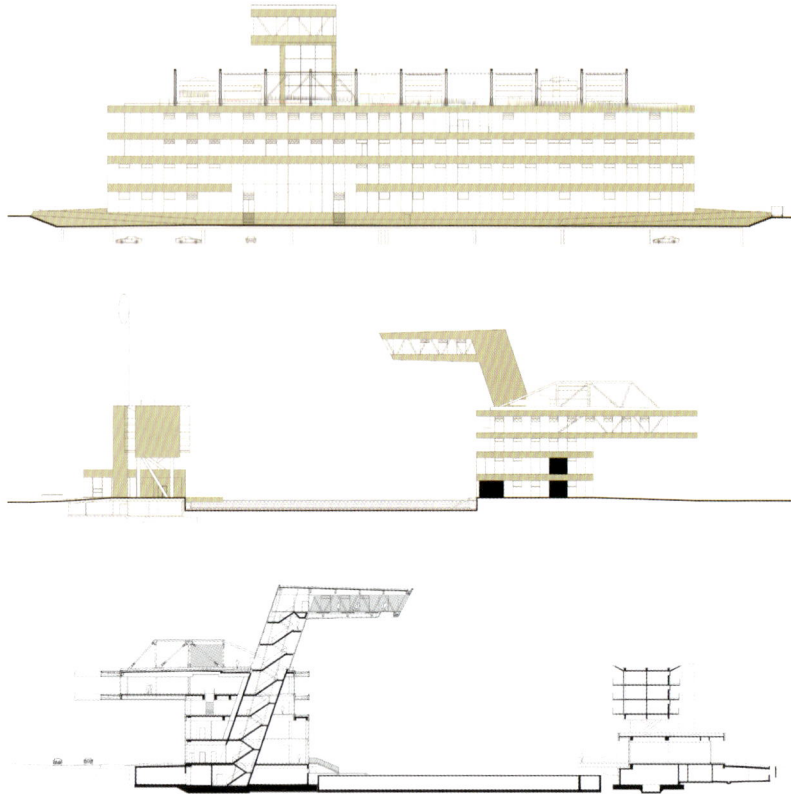

The "New Centre of Lehen" project is a dominant piece of architecture surrounded by largely insignificant buildings. Concerning urban space, the district has been given a completely new identity and the opportunity to start to develop a new self-consciousness through this project. The new facilities are reminiscent of the old Lehen stadium, whereby, the playing surfaces have a similar structure and present people with a certain sense of nostalgia. The use of the slanted tower with the Panorama Bar could be described as an emblematic support for this retrospection.

The architectural language of the project meets high international standards in its liberality and its memorable power of organisation and task definition. The implementation of a constructive design is especially unique and its form developed exclusively based on the location, the interpretation of its history and the given tasks.

The old stadium in Lehen has been transformed. The essential centre of a stadium, the playing field, this great empty green surface, presents the central content and the actual value for the utilisation and, as a tribute, was kept at the same size and made into a peaceful public park with an "English lawn", accessible to the general public.

The sparse features preserve the character of a generous, noble lawn surface which, as a kind of green lung in the centre of Lehen, is a contrasting place of relaxation to be seen and reachable from all sides and in contrast to the pulsating drive all around it. As a central element, this open space mediates between the commercial, social and sacral facilities. The idiom of the enthusiasm/disappointment felt watching a football match is interpreted into a contemplative view of a park to which the viewer is draw because it promises relaxation and reconciliation. All the buildings on the park side are completely covered in glass and have generous verandas, terraces and loggias reminiscent of stand boxes to keep the events alive and give the archetypical observer the chance to participate in them.

1. In the eastern part of "Neue Mitte Lehen"
2. The entrance side western part of "Neue Mitte Lehen", entrance side of the library
3. The western part of "Neue Mitte Lehen" with the Panorama Bar

2

3

1. Foyer, western side, library
2. Inside the western part, the foyer of the library

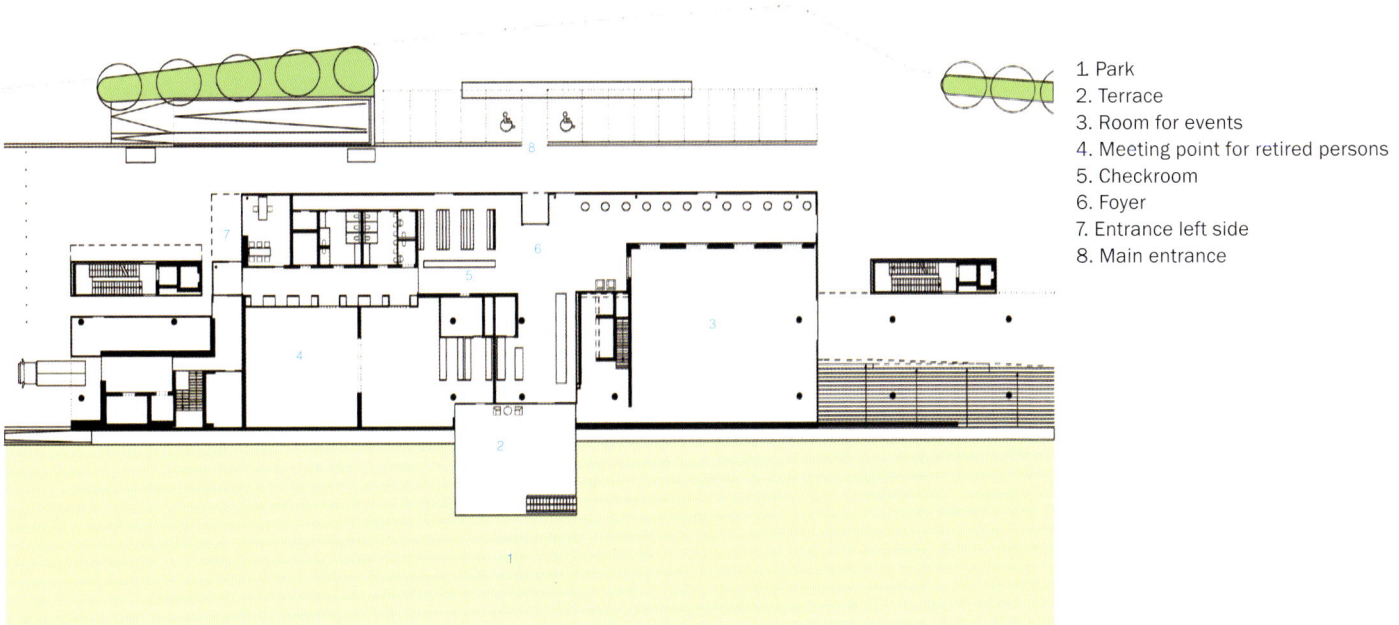

1. Park
2. Terrace
3. Room for events
4. Meeting point for retired persons
5. Checkroom
6. Foyer
7. Entrance left side
8. Main entrance

1-3. Library interior

2

3

Gabriela Mistral Cultural Centre

Location: Santiago, Chile **Designed by:** Lateral Arquitectura & Diseño **Completion date:** 2010 **Photos©:** Nicolás Saieh **Area:** 44,000 sqm

A building for arts and culture should always be varying degrees of transparency and not only share and engage users directly but also to the whole community. Therefore, the architects opted for a design that provided openness within the public spaces and transparency into the interior spaces. The halls for the performing arts of music, dance, and theatre, are on display to the public as "boxes or containers."

Horizontally the building is organised around three volumes that contain and represent the three major programme areas. These are the Documentation Centre for the Performing Arts and Music, the Training Room of the Performing Arts, and the Great Hall Theatre seating 2,000 people. The three buildings are separate at street level providing multiple covered pedestrian spaces. At the lower levels all three buildings are directly connected.

The main materials that make up the building are all possible to find in the original building with five design elements that are worth noting: weathering steel, reinforced concrete in sight, glass, steel, and wood. The use of the weathering steel (with holes) creates an immediate visual link between past, present, and future.

Given the specifics of the programme, each room was treated independently looking for the best acoustic comfort according to its corresponding activity. For example, the Music Hall presents a design of inclined planes and breaks that are capable of directing high quality sound to all viewers and maintaining a warm contemporary expression. The Music Hall along with the Dance Room have space for audio and lighting control located at the bottom of each chamber taking the place of the old translation booths from when it was the Building Diego Portales.

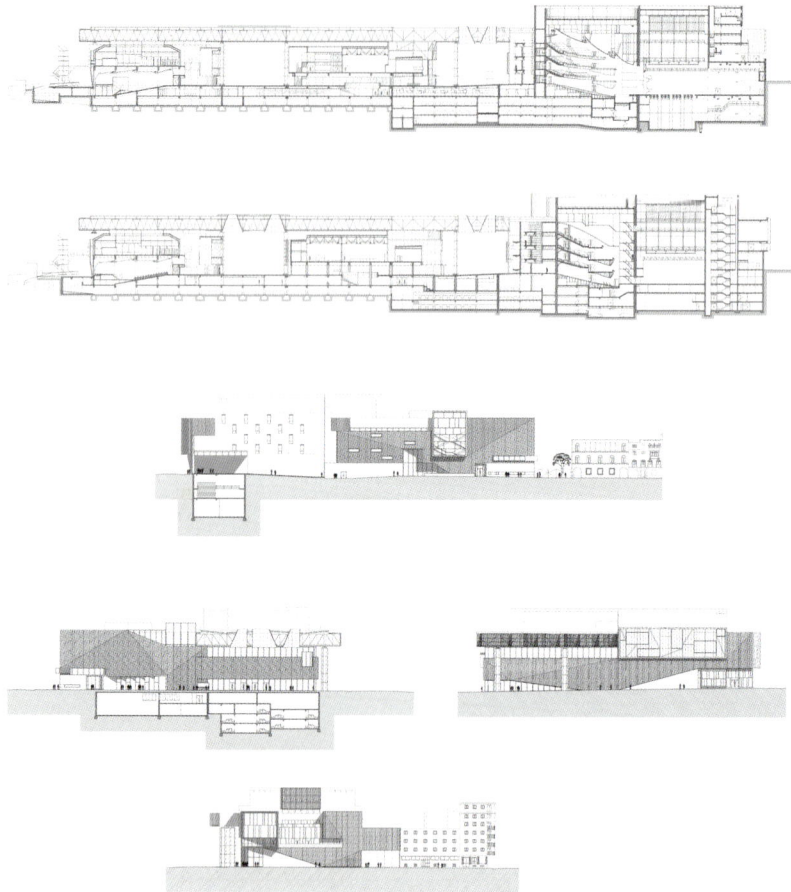

1. Back street view
2. Main entrance
3. Open terrace for lounge and connecting with the upper level

1

2

1. Weathering steel (with holes) creates special façade for the cultural centre
2. Lounge behind weathering steel (with holes) façade

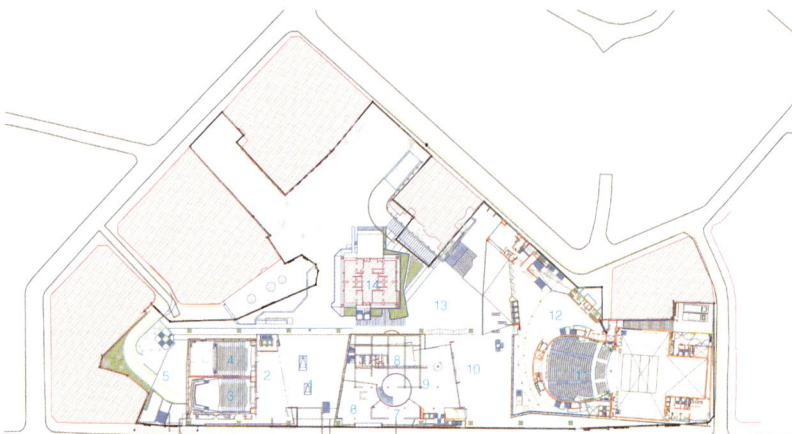

1. Covered west square access
2. Auditoriums hall
3. Auditorium 1
4. Auditorium 2
5. Subway side access
6. Store 1
7. Store 2
8. Coffee shop
9. Access hall 2 building
10. Covered east square
11. Theatre
12. Theatre's hall
13. Buried backyard
14. Pre-existing building

1. Central atrium under special designed roof
2. Main entrance to the volume
3. Interior hallway
4. The Great Hall Theatre

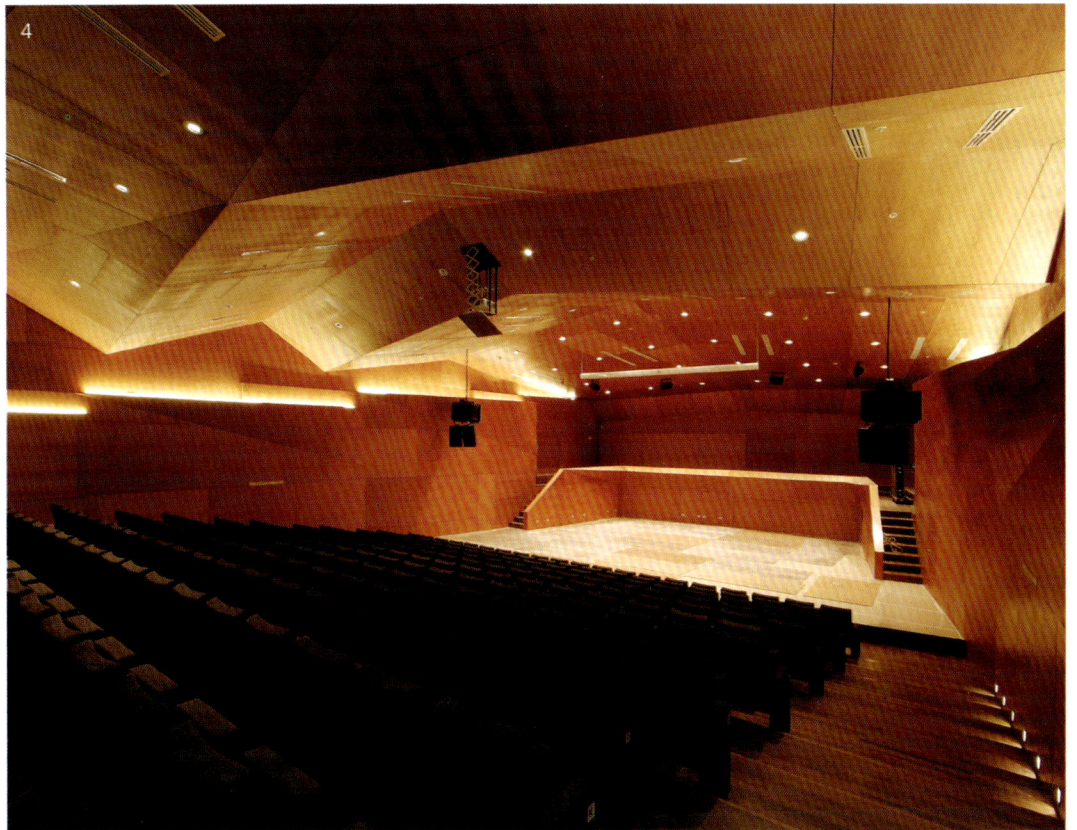

Sjakket

Location: Copenhagen, Denmark **Designed by:** JDS Architects **Completion date:** 2008 **Photos©:** Felix Luong, Vegar Moen, JDS Architects **Award:** 2008 Contract World Award for Best Educational/ Learning/Cultural Facility

The Sjakket project involved the conversion of a former factory building into a cultural centre for young people. This is a social project undertaken in the industrial north-west part of Copenhagen, which has a large immigrant population. The building not only offers the local youth a meeting place with a well-meaning, but also is a high-minded programme of cultural improvement. Sjakket speaks the language of the streets and makes a bold statement.

The architects decided not to remove the graffiti on the outside walls, but to take them seriously and use them as inspiration for the building's colour scheme. The raw industrial architecture has not been prettified: indeed, the same rawness is deliberately echoed in a striking new addition. Thus the project revitalised the existing building.

The designer gutted one of the vaulted buildings in order to allow space for a vast sports hall, and then organised the smaller, more intimate programmes into the second half. A large garage door installation also allows the south side to open into the courtyard, acting as an extension into the urban realm. Within the existing "canyon" between the two vaulted roofs a secret oasis of sorts was conceived as a roof deck. Above this space, the studio of Ghetto Noize Records is located in an industrial shipping container, spanning the two peaks. This exists as the only architectural addition to the massing of the building and has become an icon of Sjakket's presence on the industrial skyline of northwest Copenhagen. This structure echoes the containers in the nearby port and makes a bold statement on the Copenhagen skyline.

Inside the building, the facilities provided by this new meeting place are attuned to the needs of its young clientele, with a sports hall, a bathing area, a recording studio and numerous smaller spaces for more intimate gatherings.

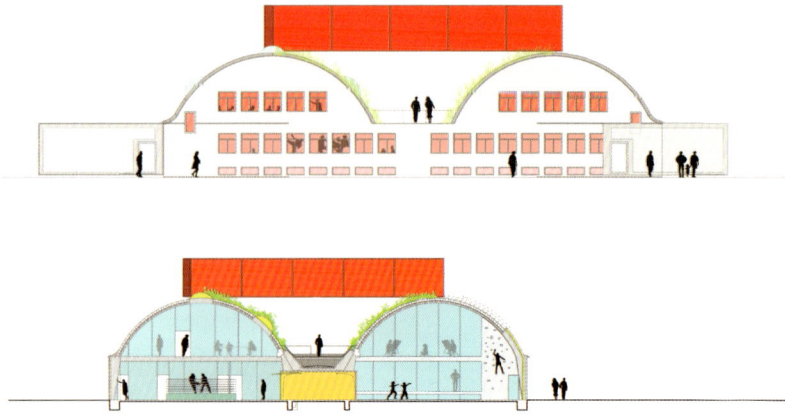

1. The graffiti on the outside walls were not removed and been taken as colour theme of the renovated building
2. Distant view of the building
3-4. Within the existing "canyon" between the two vaulted roofs a secret oasis of sorts was conceived as a roof deck. Above this space, the studio of Ghetto Noize Records is located in an industrial shipping container, spanning the two peaks

1

2

3

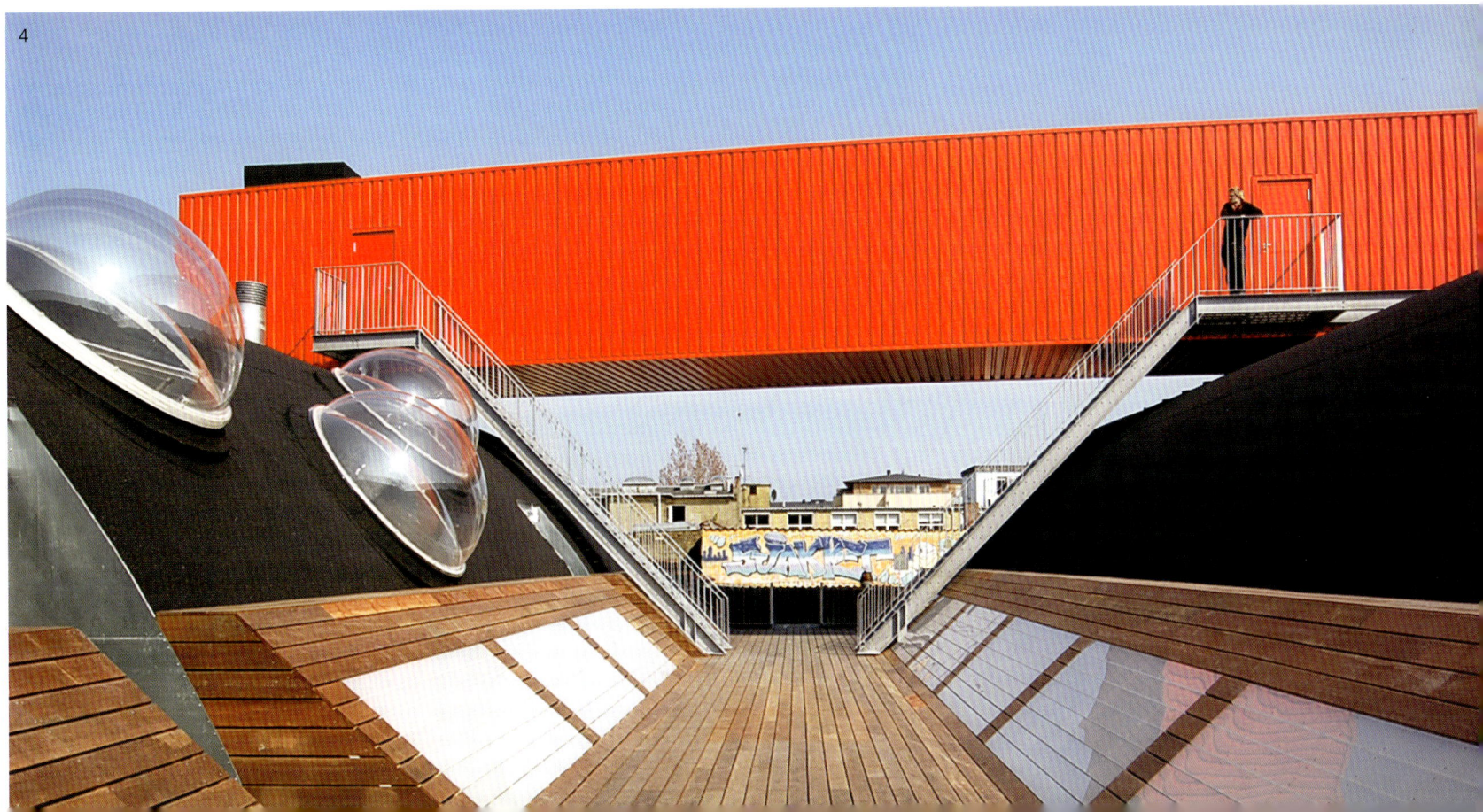

4

1. The former factory building reborn with young life
2. Sports hall inside
3. Meeting/gathering space

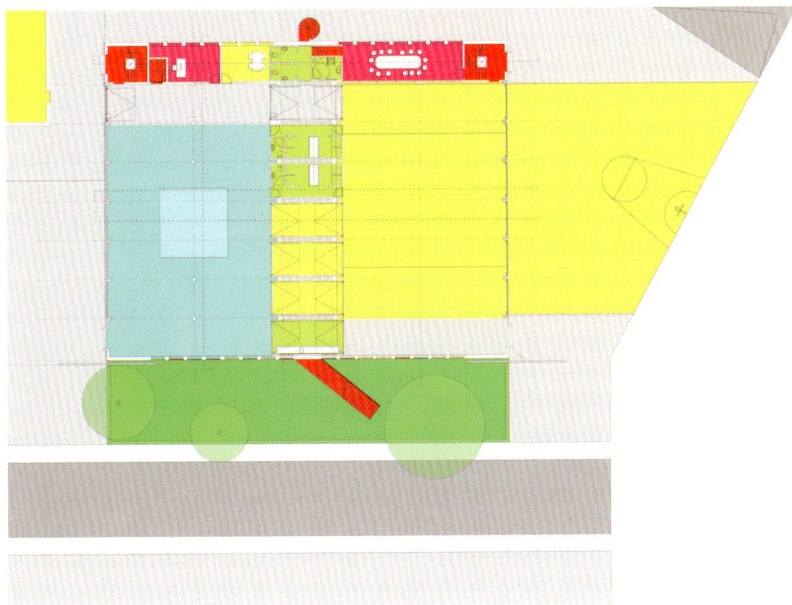

Ground floor plan

First floor plan

1. Public and intimate space combined in one space
2. Hallway with glass curtain wall also provides good view of the outer surroundings

1. The new world for the youth to think and create
2. Bathing room
3. Foyer connecting to numerous spaces for intimate gathering

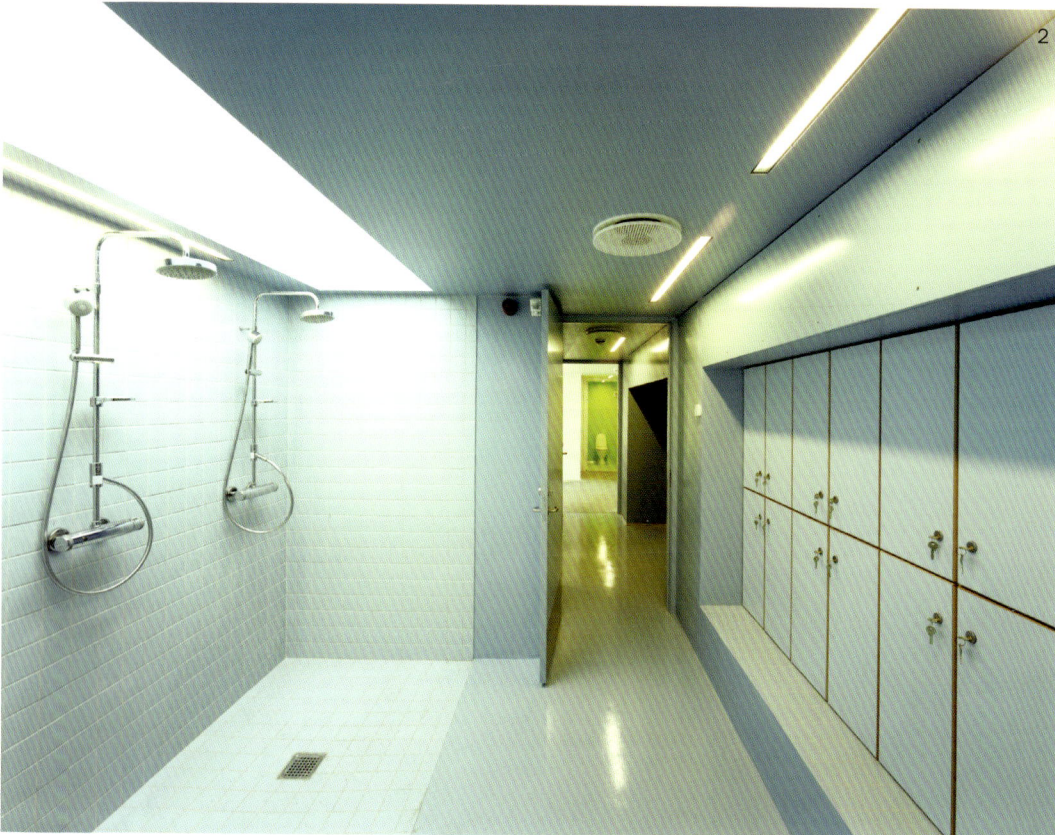

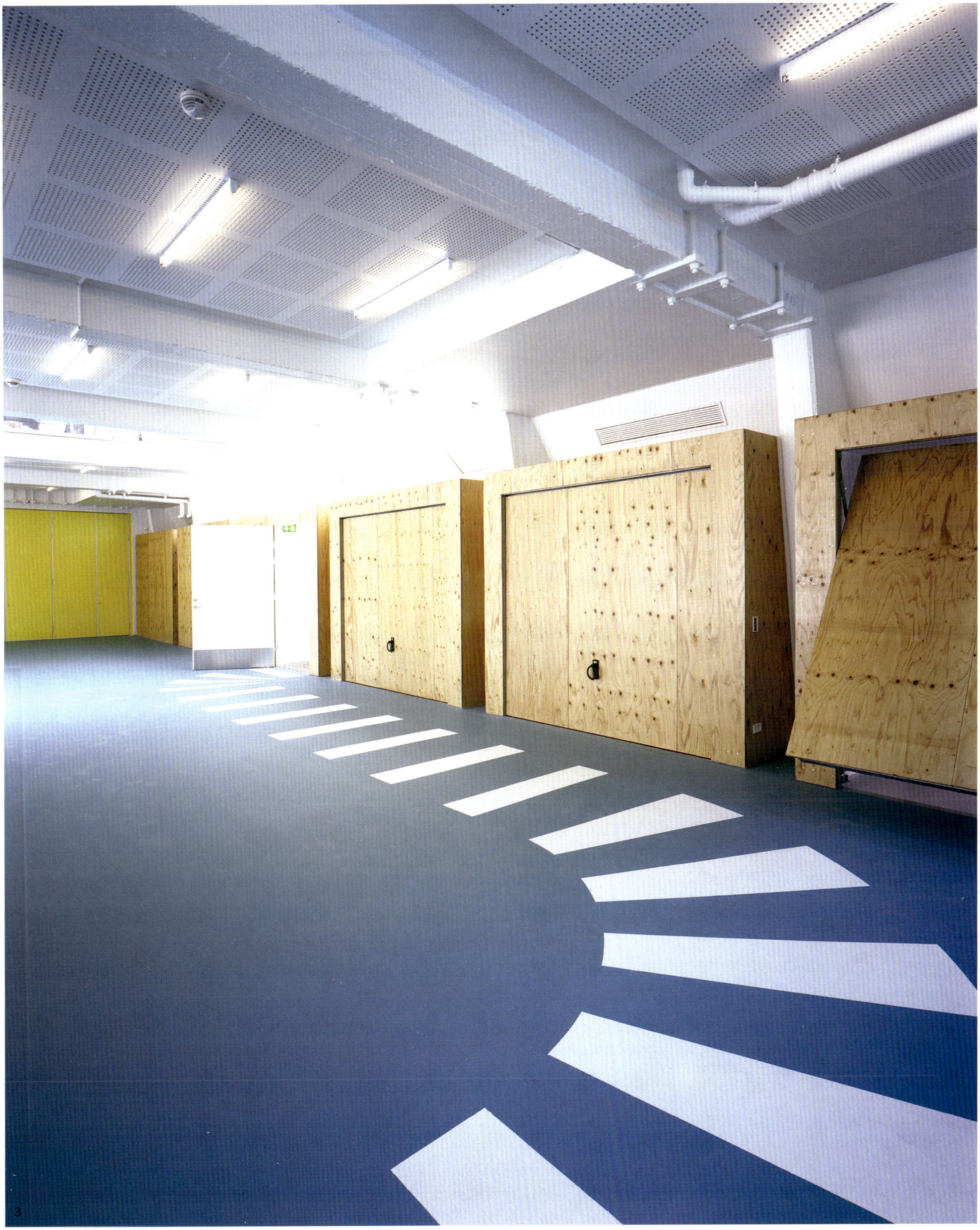

3

Cultural Centre Miguel Delibes

Location: Valladolid, Spain **Designed by:** Ricardo Boll Taller de Arquitectura **Completion Date:** 2007
Photos©: Carlos Casariego **Award:** Spanish Architecture Awards-Category Winner, 2008

The project of the Cultural Centre Miguel Delibes is presented as "a city of art within the city" and that goal is being met with operating schools and the different and varied programmes of activities in the three rooms.

The architectural design of such facilities is complex, given that it is a surface of 54,000 square metres, which combine the various disciplines (training, auditioning, performing arts, public and academic functions). The architects think it could be very interesting from the standpoint of performance-and-teaching-mixing professionals (musicians, choreographers, dancers, etc) training school students, as they are professionals in the future.

The set is a large open space inside which is located some steps "boxes" (chamber hall, auditorium and experimental theatre), along with their relevant schools (conservatory of music, drama schools and dance school). Its three most important elements are the structure due to the great lights, sound and scenery. In these three sections has worked with national and international teams due to the large size of the work. One of the most important issues for the architects was the acoustics. It had to be impeccable and this has conditioned many of the materials part of the Boards of both the coverings and ceilings as furniture.

From the point of view of sustainability Miguel Delibes Cultural Centre is equipped with a lighting time management to ensure that no misuse of it. To reduce water use, plumbing fixtures are equipped with mechanisms for eco-efficiency (two tanks downloads, fluxores, water-saving buttons ...). The air conditioning vent is recovered by the energy that is expelled to the outside from the room returning a portion of this using the recoil energy enthalpy.

1. General night view
2. Main entrance
3. General day view

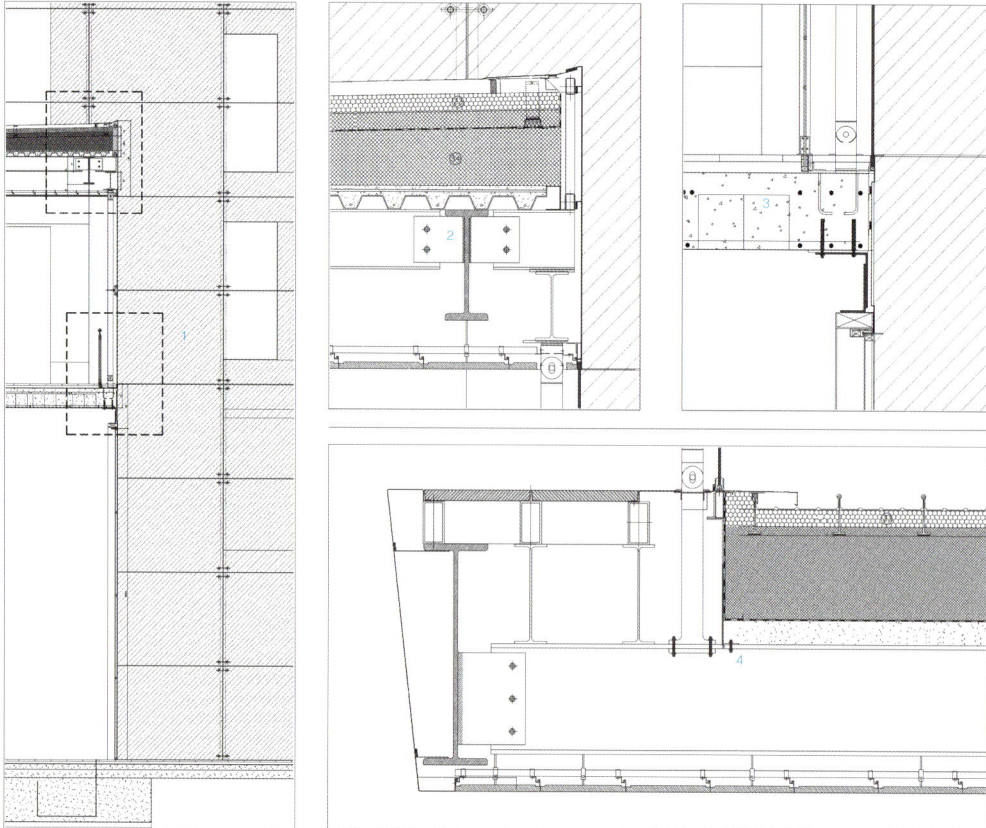

1. Public and academic space
2. Training space
3. Performing arts centre
4. Audition area

1. Theatre's interior view
2. Main Concert Hall's view

1. Theatre's interior view
2. Main Concert Hall's view

Docks of Paris

Location: Paris, France **Designed by:** JAKOB+MACFARLANE **Completion date:** 2009 **Photos©:** JAKOB+MACFARLANE **Award:** 2009 Mies van der Rohe Award

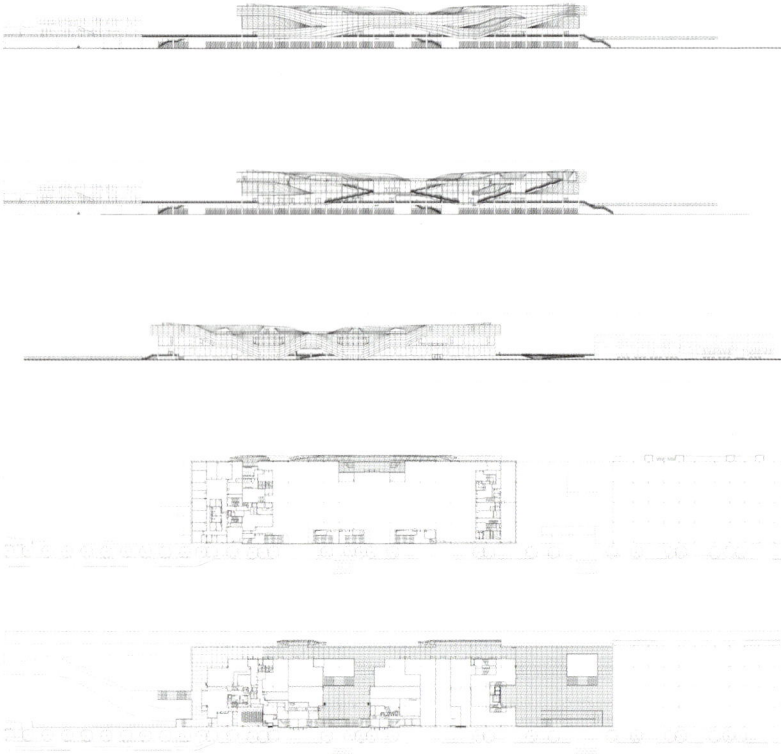

Jakob+MacFarlane opted to retain the existing structure and used it to form and influence the new project. The existing structure was built in 1907 as an industrial warehouse facility for the Port of Paris, and was the first reinforced concrete building in Paris. The three-storey structure was conceived as a series of four pavilions, each with one 10-metre wide bay and four 7.5-metre wide bays.

The concept of the new project is known as a "Plug-Over". Here, the idea was to create a new external skin that is inspired primarily by the flux of the Seine and the promenades along the sides of the river banks. The skin both protects the existing structure and forms a new layer containing most of the public circulation systems and added programme, as well as creating a new top floor to the existing building.

The new structural system supporting this skin is the result of a systematic deformation of the existing conceptual grid of the docks building. An arborescent generating method is used to create a new system from the existing system, that is, "growing" the new building from the old as new branches grow on a tree. This skin is created principally from a glass exterior skin, steel structure, wood decking and grassed, faceted roofscape.

The "Plug-Over" operates not only as a way of exploiting the maximum building envelope but enables a continuous public path to move up through the building from the lowest level alongside the Seine to the roof deck and back down, a kind of continuous loop enabling the building to become part of the urban condition.

The programme is a rich mix centred on the themes of design and fashion, including exhibition spaces, the French Fashion Institute (IFM), music producers, bookshops, cafes, and a restaurant.

1. General day view from distance
2. Façade night view detail

1

1, 2. River side terrace
3. Roof terrace detail

3

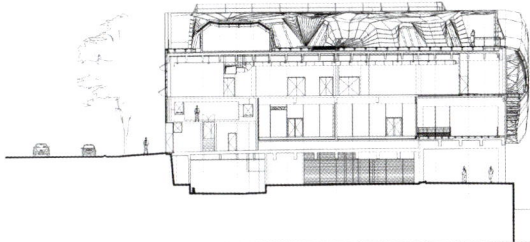

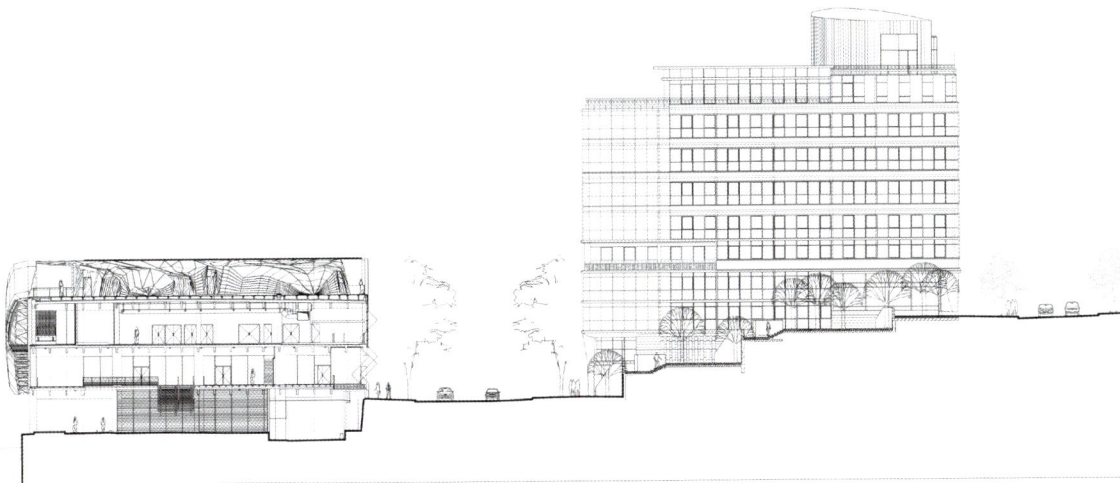

1. Façade structure detail
2. Hallway inside behind the façade
3. French window brings great view of the river

Zhongguancun Cultural Centre

Location: Beijing, China **Designed by:** gmp – von Gerkan, Marg and Partners Architects **Completion date:** 2006 **Photos©:** Christian Gahl, Ben McMillan

The development of the former "Haidian Book City" to an ultramodern cultural forum lastingly gives an impression of future Beijing. In this connection the Zhongguancun Media Tower is of particular significance due to its location on the 4th Ring Road.

It is the overall approach to reflect the requirement of multimedia communication in the appearance of the building and to design it extremely efficient at the same time. In this context the form of the building accommodates complex influences of the surroundings. For this reason the trapezoidal plan follows the historical diagonal connection.

The public areas of the building are accessed via a mall in the north-south direction, which offers a generous gallery space on the first six floors. By means of deep, swung cuts in the façade pedestrians are invited to enter the building via the northern plaza. From here they enter in the department stores and shops placed in the ground floor and the first floor. In contrast to this public access the internal entrance to the building opens effectively to the eastern road with generous drop off zone. The V-shaped space orientated to the road evokes a breathtaking and unique atmosphere, which is still increased by light and sound installations. The employees reach the lobby on the first floor directly via escalators. This lobby serves as an access zone to the lifts, and is independent of the mall.

The form of the building is aligned to the requirements of modern work, particularly in media business. The wide office areas in the eastern part are especially suited for team work with high flexibility, while in the office areas in the west are designed for concentrated work in separated offices. Due to the depth of these wings of 15 metres group offices can be alternatively allocated. Furthermore the plan permits highly efficient divisibility of the total floor areas of maximum 9 units.

The roof level is designed as a business centre with elegant restaurants, bars, discotheques and terraces. Due to the building height of 80 metres visitors enjoy a great panorama view over Beijing.

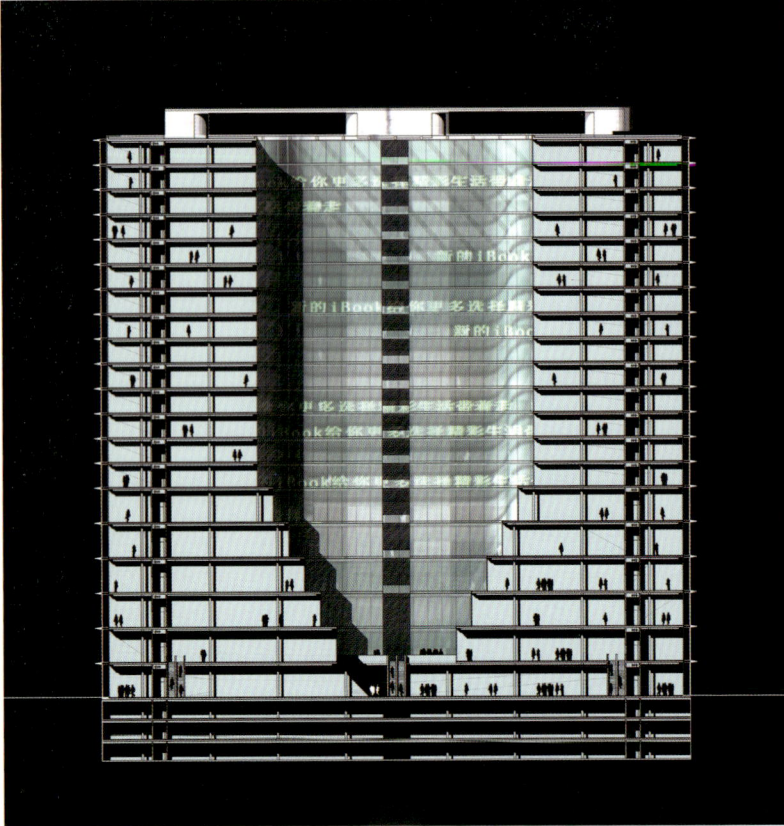

1. General day view
2. General night view

1, 2. Atrium

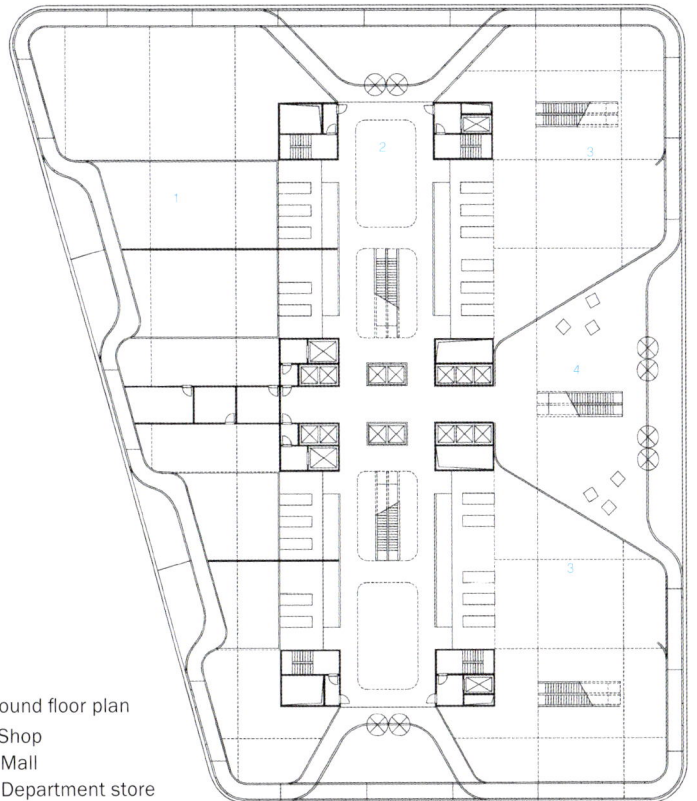

Ground floor plan
1. Shop
2. Mall
3. Department store
4. Access office

Regional Cultural Centre Letterkenny

Location: Letterkenny, Ireland **Designed by:** MacGabhann Architects **Completion date:** 2007 **Photos**©: Dennis Gilbert **Construction area:** 1,800 sqm **Awards:** Opus Between 2 Million & 20 Million Award, OPUS Architecture & Construction Awards 2008, Shortlisted for Galvanising Awards 2009, Architectural Association of Ireland Awards 2009 – Special Mention

The location of the building – set back from two main streets on the inside of a deep site and stuck between the An Griannan Theatre and the Leisure Centre – required a special approach to its form and its façade. As it is not located on a street edge there was a chance to create a new layer of urban structure, i.e. a new footpath connecting the two existing roads and giving Letterkenny not only a new building but a new patch of urban (infra) structure.

The Regional Cultural Centre is visible from different places in town. It makes itself visible through the big cantilevered gallery box acting as a modern day obelisk announcing the existence of something important on that slightly hidden so far "undiscovered" plot behind the theatre. Due to its direction the cantilever guides visitors and pedestrians approaching from the swimming pool to the entrance of the building – or further to the Port Road.

The cantilevered box contains the most important part of the building, the Art Gallery. This is made visible in the city through the golden wall that emerges from within the building covering a complete side of the gallery. Facing west it reflects the evening light and provides a golden glow on the ground at the entrance. This 270-square-metre gallery provides ample high-spec exhibition space. Two large skylights extruding over the roof of the building and a flexible lighting system ensure the best light conditions for different exhibition types.

The building is communicating to its surrounding in many ways. The proscenium stage-like two-storey foyer with its fully glazed front, acts as an intermediate space between art and public. With its back wall designed to facilitate changing exhibitions, the contact of the passing public and the institution of art becomes literally unavoidable, thus breaking down an often-existing invisible barrier between the two.

1. North and west façades showing Workshop 3 and office skylight glazing
2. South façade showing entrance
3. View from the Port Road
4. West elevation

3

4

1. Ramp leading to entrance
2. Gallery
3. View from the top of sky stairs

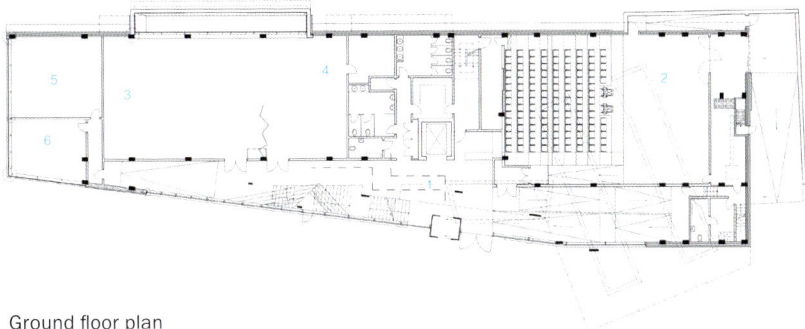

Ground floor plan
1. Foyer
2. Theatre
3. Workshop 1
4. Workshop 2
5. Multimedia suite
6. Animation studio

Cultural Centre Bafile

Location: Caorle VE, Italy **Designed by:** Studio Macola **Completion date:** 2009 **Photos©:** Marco Zanta
Floor area: 8,600 sqm

Since the 1930s, the former school "Bafile" has played a central role in the modernisation of Caorle's suburbs. Besides providing essential services, the school complex has shaped decisively the surrounding landscape, dictating and orienting the pace of urban expansion over several decades.

The present restoration project is part of an overall plan intended to redesign the town's historical city centre. Promoted by the Caorle Council, the plan consists of three separate spheres of architectural intervention with target: the religious and monumental complex centred on the Duomo, the administrative and managerial complex revolving around the former town hall, and the "Bafile" area, which will now be devoted to a variety of socio-cultural activities.

The "Bafile" project is above all defined by its use of empty spaces and, most notably, by the creation of a new pedestrian square – or "piazza" – connected to the historical city centre. The volumes thus brought into being transformed and supplemented the original architectural typology of the "Bafile" complex. The project enhances the architectural role of the former school's cylindrical hall, which constitutes one of the termini of the town's main pedestrian thoroughfare and serves to delimit the southern boundaries of the new piazza. On the opposite side, the square is demarcated by the newly built theatre and library, which are now organic parts of the redesigned city centre.

The compact structure and brick façade of the theatre underscore its valuable public role and unique importance in the overall economy of the project. The façade of the library overlooking the square comprises a porch sheltering glass wall whose transparency bring about a close, "open" relationship between the inside and the outside of the building. The structure of the Multimedia Centre permits it to host separate events and activities at the same time. An elongated single hall joins its exhibition rooms, the theatre and the library. This architectural solution enables each component of the Centre to act independently while preserving the overall unity of the Centre itself.

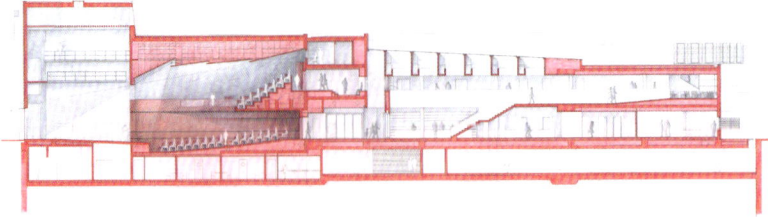

1. Theatre front
2. Offices entrance
3. Kids centre

1. Office exterior
2. Room
3. Staircase

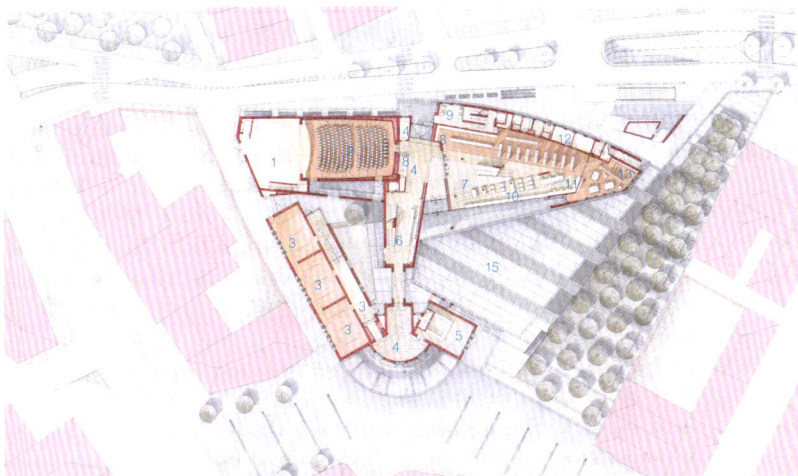

1. Stage
2. Theatre of 300 seats
3. Gallery
4. Main lobby
5. Bar
6. Cloakroom
7. Library
8. Information
9. Offices entrance
10. Newspaper
11. Internet point
12. Offices
13. Kids area
14. Tickets office
15. Plaza

New Jiangwan Culture Centre

Location: Shanghai, China **Designed by:** RTKL **Completion date:** 2007 **Photos©:** RTKL

Located in Shanghai, New Jiangwan Town is a model for a sustainable community for the 21st Century. The area's culture centre, located in a central park, was designed to celebrate and showcase the environmental sensitivity and community-oriented feel of the new town with 6,000 sqaure metres of exhibition, education, performance, leisure and entertainment facilities across two floors. The culture centre provides a fluid interaction between interior and exterior spaces. The horizontal building is highly integrated with the landscape and nature.

The building encourages and stimulates public access and interactions within its dynamic spaces. Organic and inorganic material palettes contrast to celebrate the fusion of man and the environment.

1. Façade detail
2. Entrance

1. Interior ceiling detail
2. Hallway

1. Peter Jay Sharp Theatre
2. Box office
3. Piano Maintenance Tech.
4. Green room
5. Admissions
6. Paul Recital Hall
7. Women's toilet
8. Men's toilet
9. Evening division
10. Alice Tully Hall
11. Bookstore

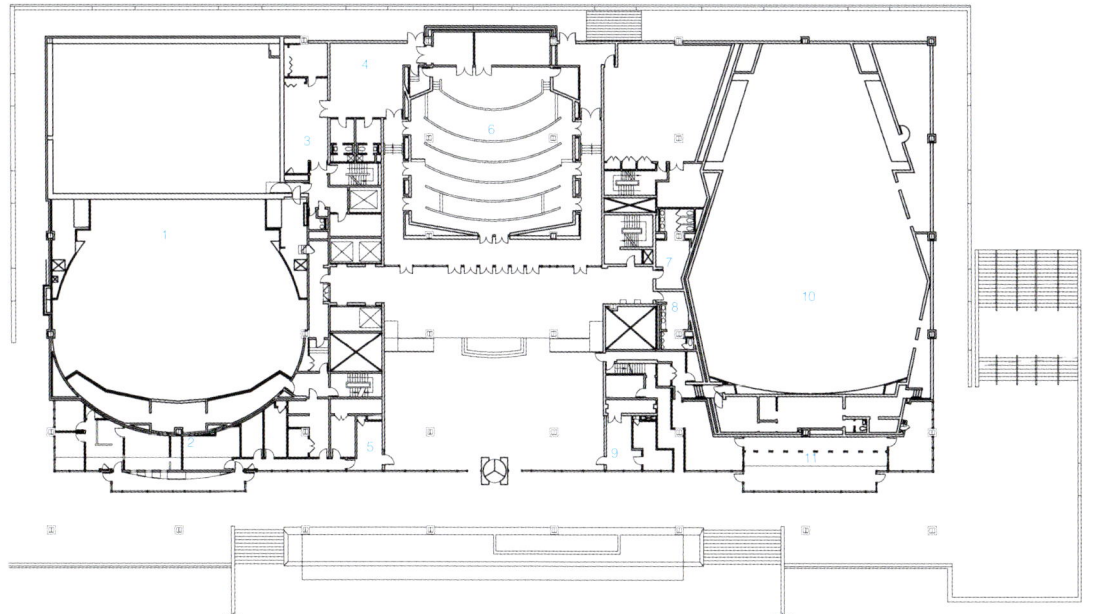

1. Hallway
2. Auditorium
3. Interior wall detail

Rio Salado Audubon Centre

Location: Arizona, USA **Designed by:** Philip Weddle **Completion date:** 2009 **Photos©:** Bill Timmerman, Chris Brown **Construction area:** 697 sqm **Awards:** AIA Western Mountain Region Honour Award 2010, AIA Arizona SRP Sustainable Award 2010, USGBC LEED Platinum Certication

The Rio Salado Audubon Centre is an Interpretive Centre/Nature Centre developed by the National Audubon Society in partnership with the City of Phoenix strategically located in the multi-cultural heart of the City to provide nature-based education to the most urban residential neighbourhoods.

The Audubon Centre is designed to choreograph the visitor's experience by sequencing and framing views. The visitor enters the Centre by passing through a mesquite bosque to an entry court. Canted weathered steel walls create a canyon like passage leading to the entry. From there visitor's views open north to the wetland, the river corridor and the city's skyline beyond. Sliding glass doors pocket to open the space to the view terrace creating a true indoor/outdoor space.

The long, low east-west orientation reduces heat gain. The building shuts itself off to the hot southern sun while opening to the northern light and views. Thoughtful window placement and sizing provides over 85% of the building's regularly occupied spaces with enough daylight that artificial light is unnecessary for most daily tasks. 100% of all regularly occupied spaces have visual connection to the outdoors: the entry courtyard, the hummingbird garden, and/or the wetland.

The centre includes an interactive nature conservancy exhibition as well as a multi-purpose learning centre for community use. The exhibition space introduces several of the on-site interpretive trails to best provide opportunities for self-directed learning and exploration. The project includes an integrated 20-kilowatt photovoltaic solar system that generates approximately 50% of the energy needed for the Centre's operation. Waste water is treated through an innovative on-site treatment system allowing for all treated water to be utilised on-site for landscape irrigation. The Audubon Centre received USGBC LEED Platinum certification due in large part to the sustainable systems that integrated into the project.

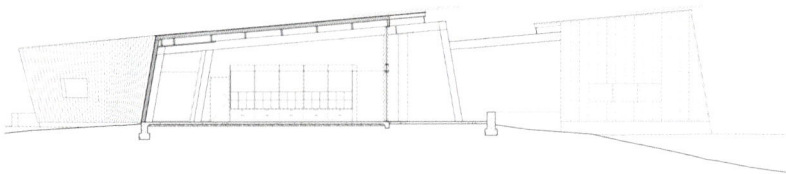

1. View of looking over wetland back at the Centre © Bill Timmerman
2. View of looking down view-terrace © Bill Timmerman

1. View of the Library/Meeting Room – north façade © Bill Timmerman
2. View over wetland out of the Library / Meeting Room © Chris Brown
3. Entry © Bill Timmerman

1. Entry court
2. Entry
3. Reception
4. Exhibition
5. Multi-purpose room
6. Catering kitchen
7. Restroom
8. Work
9. Open office
10. Break room
11. Office
12. Meeting/library
13. View terrace

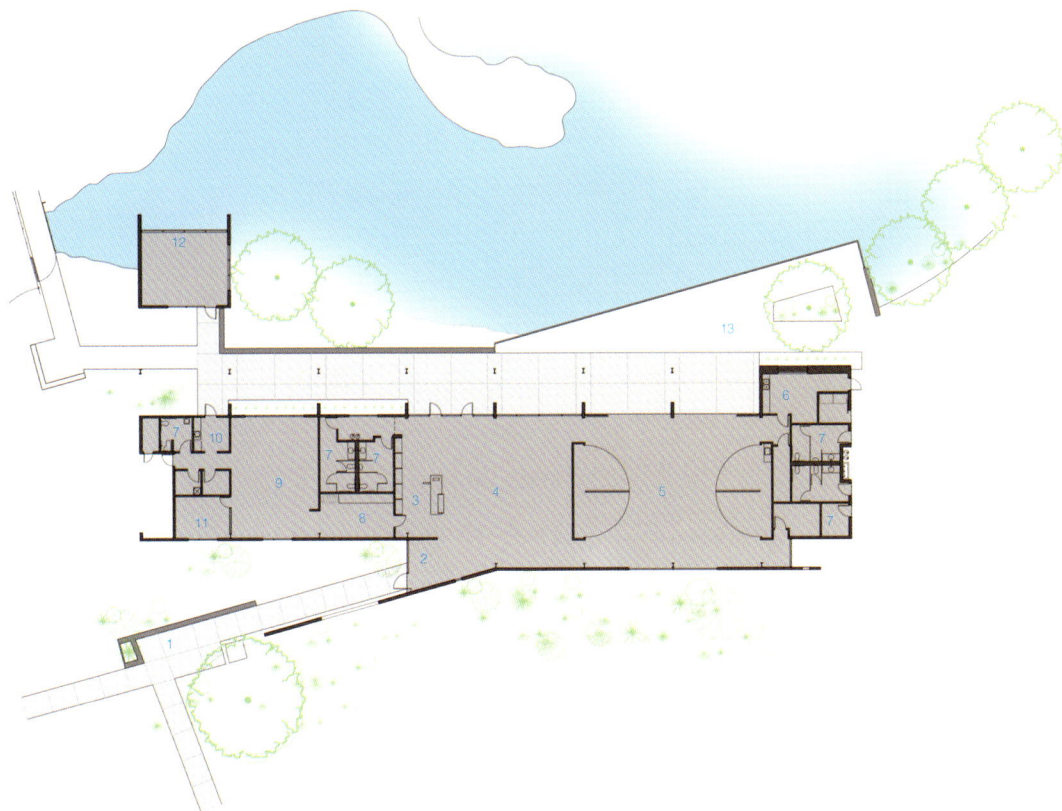

1 Exhibition space
2. Lecture hall

2

Norveg Coast Cultural Centre

Location: Rørvik, Norway **Designed by:** Gudmundur Jonsson Arkitektkontor **Completion date:** 2004
Construction area: 1,730 sqm **Photos©:** Thomas Mayer, Erco Leuchten

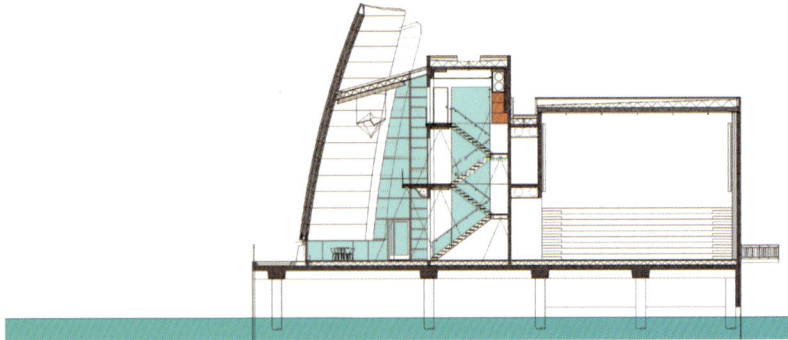

Norveg is situated in the Community Rørvik, which has long tradition for fishery, and represents the utmost of the Norwegian coastal culture through ages. Today there is a boat-building industry carrying on the tradition, but in a modern way. Being situated by the coast, Norveg represents in one way a challenge bringing visitors to the place, ensuring economic stability in the organisation of the centre. Therefore the architect stated, that a building of significance was needed to ensure attention to this community.

The architect "visited" the ancient times of fishery and used the culture for inspiration in creating the idea. Thus the idea is based on the image of three sails, which lean against a modern vessel, such uniting the sailing-boat tradition and the modern ships. The building becomes an evolution of a coast-cultural history visualised in architecture. The building even consists of an after-deck or a hind part to complete the interpretation of the ship-in heritage.

The building occupies 1,730 square metres. The organisation follows the architectural elements. The main central vessel or hull as the spine of the building houses the administration, kitchen and technical plants. The sails cover the foyer, restaurant and temporary exhibition. The big rock on the other side symbolising the shore that the ship is docking to, contains the multimedia and concert/auditorium space. At last the after-deck containing the coast-cultural exhibition is also designed by the same architect.

The height between the floor and the sails is just 140 centimetres, and this is due to the interpretation of the sailboats that have the sail boom low, and people have to bend to cross sails. In this particular case, this is also due to the reason that the architect wants people to stop, calm down and have a seat to enjoy the view to the ocean, in such way people hardly see the sea unless sitting down. The visitor is captured in the vessel, and has to experience it from the inside as well.

1. General day view
2. Side view of façade at night

1. View of front façade
2. Main entrance at winter night

2

1. Lobby café
2. Café detail

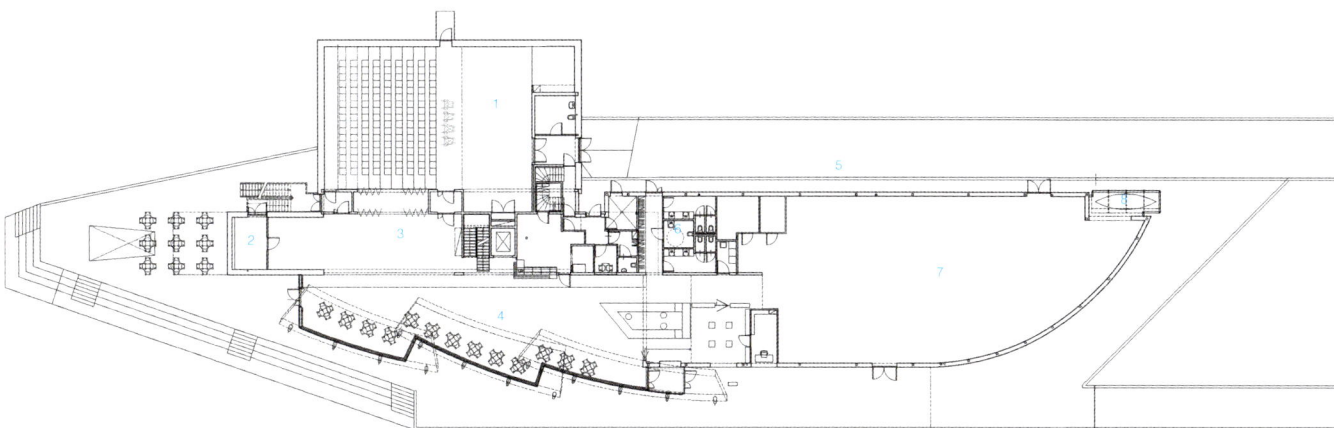

1. C-stage
2. Recliner warehouse
3. Temporary exhibition
4. Café and lounge area
5. Wooden pier/dock
6. Toilets
7. Permanent exhibition
8. Showcase

Maritime Centre Vellamo

Location: Kotka, Finland **Designed by:** Architects Lahdelma & Mahlamäki **Completion date:** 2008
Photos©: Jussi Tiainen **Floor area:** 14,601 sqm

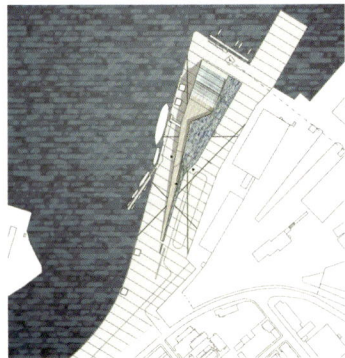

Kotka's Maritime Centre Vellamo is the beacon of the cityscape. The figure guides travellers from the city into a harbour of culture. The Old Harbour will soon be transformed into a Culture Harbour. As the first building completed the Maritime Centre will be the functional cornerstone of the area.

References to the sea incorporated in the building's distinctive architecture link the Maritime Centre to the sea and also to the features of the Kymenlaakso region. The abstract image of a large wave creates a physical representation of the sea. Situated at the end of the planned culture harbour, the roof of the Maritime Centre forms a square, which will play host to a wide array of different events.

The interior of the Maritime Centre is characterised by the application of timeless architectural concepts. The entrance, the foyer and the elevated, centrally located exhibition hall give the interior of the Maritime Centre its distinctive character; together they form a spatial entity fashioned from free-shaped wall faces, a material world dominated by oak-wood surfaces and the expanding nature of the surrounding space.

The Maritime Centre is home to two permanent residents: the Maritime Museum of Finland and the Museum of Kymenlaakso. There are also a museum shop, a restaurant, a library, seminar and teaching rooms and a 250-seat auditorium.

The elevated exhibition space housing the permanent collection, plays a key role. The exhibition rooms have been designed to make them as adaptable as possible. The clearly defined shapes and proportions of these rooms, the neutral grey colouring specified on all surfaces and fittings make them suitable for housing a whole host of different museum exhibitions.

The Maritime Centre is primarily built around a column and beam system of reinforced concrete girders. The floors consist largely of structural hollow-core slabs, while the walkway on the roof is designed as an inverted structure. The outer walls are constructed using a lightweight skeleton structure. Sheet-metal cassettes, painted in a variety of different shades, are the primary building material on the exterior of the building, to which a lattice made of aluminium and pressed-silk glass has been affixed.

1. View of front façade
2. Side view

1. Side view of façade
2. Entry lobby
3. Hallway

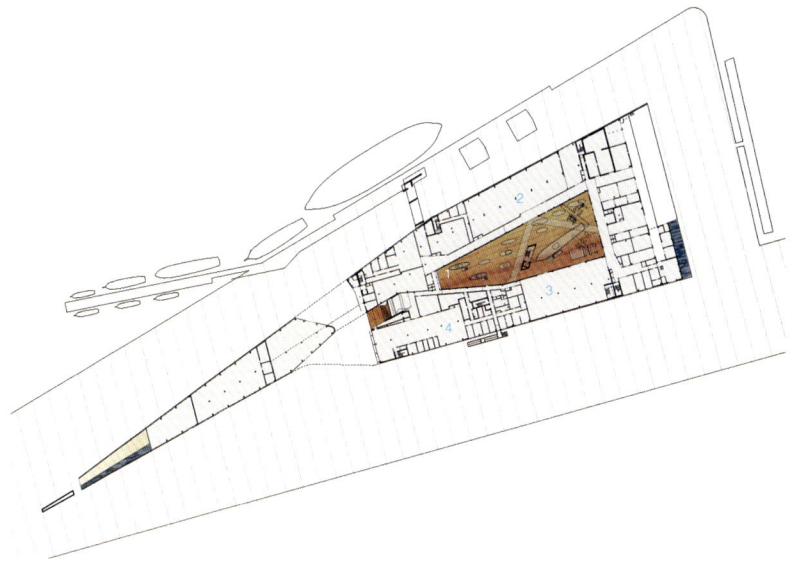

1. Exhibition
2. Hall
3. Hall
4. Room

1. Exhibition space
2. Hall

Location: Jalisco, México. **Designed by:** Heriberto Hernández Ochoa, Raúl Juárez Perezlete, Jorge Hernández Luquín **Completion date:** 2007 **Photos©:** Heriberto Hernández Ochoa **Area:** 5,346 sqm

Library and Media Centre for the University of Guadalajara

This building is a pioneer in the implementation of standardised norms for accessibility for people with disabilities; it has a set of ramps and aisles specially designed to make it 100% accessible. It will have a collection of 120,000 books, DVDs, and videos in a total surface of 5,346 square metres, making it the biggest public library in the western region of Mexico, and the second one after the recently opened Central Library Jose Vasconcelos in Mexico.

It was impossible for them to design a library and media centre at the beginning of the 21st century as these typologies have been designed for the past 20 or 30 years, the architects felt the urge to make a statement about a time that, perhaps, was about to change. The process in itself involved a series of playful strategies in order to let the authorship of the process aside, the architects wanted randomness in the process, the architects desired to lay some rules and let the whole thing play itself.

The building is designed as three elements that intersect at the point of intersection are the main lobby, front desk and informal reading areas. One of the elements is a concrete volume that protects the whole collection of the library. From the outside this concrete box is completely closed and without any openings. At the main lobby the concrete dematerialises into a steel structure that shows the stacks of books.

The user is confronted to this wall of books as he enters the main space of the library. The other two elements that intersect at the lobby are the reading areas, which are built in red brick, and the media centre is clad in metal. The different materials or these elements make it clear to the user that there are different programmes inside, and that each element has a distinctive programme: the reading areas are in the red brick element, the media centre in the metal clad volume and the books in the concrete box.

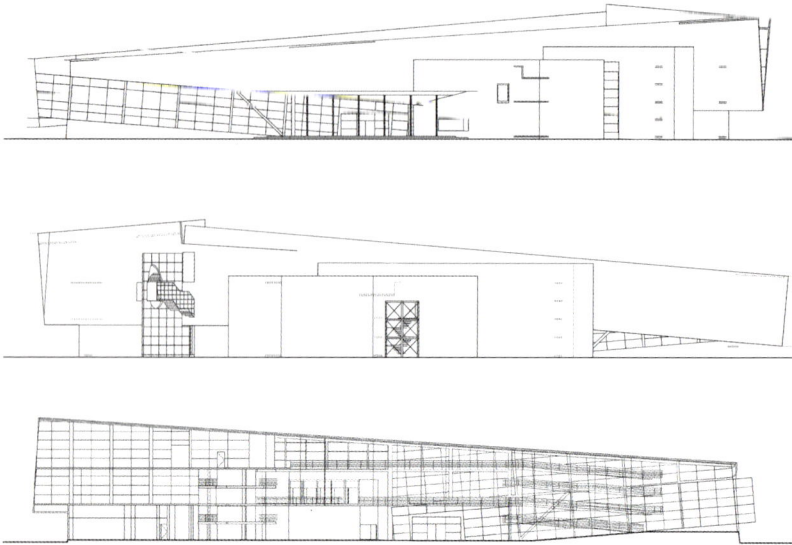

1. Ramps volume detail
2. Main entrance from the east
3. Main façade from plaza
4. Ramps volume

1

2

3

4

1

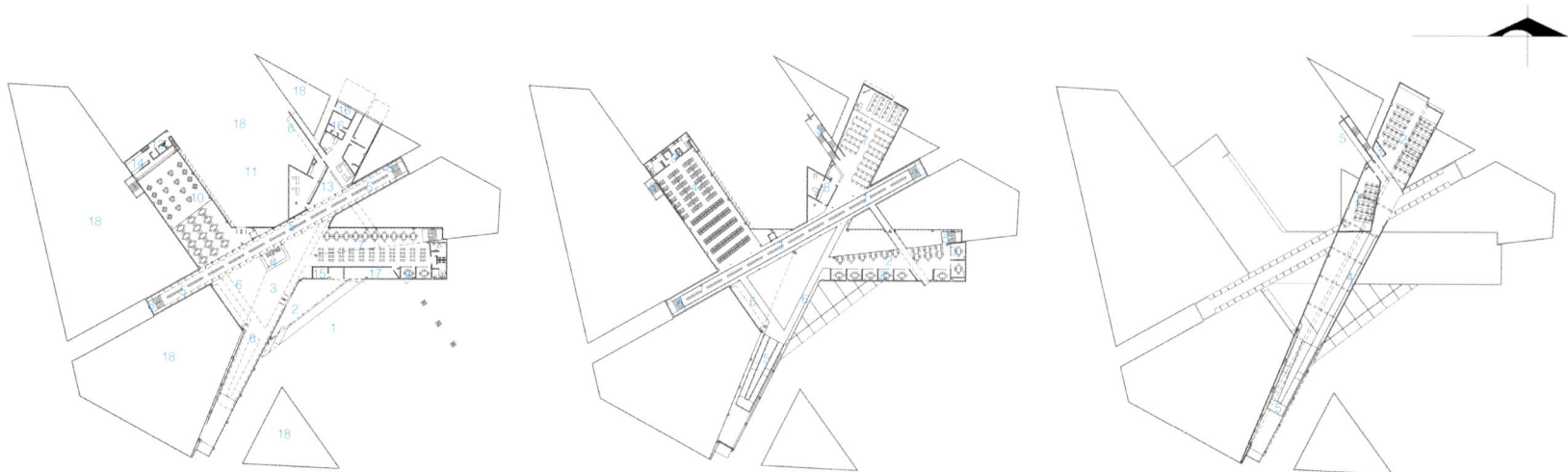

1. Plaza
2. Entrance
3. Main lobby
4. Front desk
5. Book shelves
6. Casual reading area
7. Reading area
8. Ramps and stairs
9. Cubicles
10. Snack area
11. Reading plaza
12. Toilets
13. Administration
14. Kitchen
15. Copy centre
16. Service
17. Lockers
18. Green areas

1. Book shelves
2. Reading area
3. Cubicles
4. Individual cubicles
5. Ramps and stairs
6. Hanging corridors
7. Multi-media centre
8. Administration
9. Toilets

1. Languages area
2. Video conference area
3. Media classroom
4. Hanging corridors
5. Ramps and stairs

1 Mediateque volume
2. Main lobby viewed from mediatheque

1. Wall of books and reading area viewed from hanging corridor
2. Interior patio
3. Ramps
4. Bridge connecting the book shelves wall to a reading area

Jacob and Wilhelm Grimm Centre

Location: Berlin, Germany **Designed by:** Max Dudler (Andreas Enge, Jochen Soydan, Andrea Deckert, Gesine Gummi) **Completion date:** 2009 **Photos©:** Stefan Mueller **Construction area:** usable service area 21,850 sqm, total surface area 37,460 sqm **Award:** Nominated, Mies Van Der Rohe Award 2011

The new Jacob and Wilhelm Grimm Centre is the largest open-shelving library in Germany and also contains the university computer centre, library administration as well as classrooms and meeting areas.

Despite the great depth of the building and the density of its interior furnishings, the library possesses a surprising porousness and openness. The source of this lies in the consistency of heights and widths throughout the building, born out in both the architecture and the furnishings. From almost any point within the building, patrons can see out of, or rather through, the building. To accommodate the desire for simple orientation, the interior of the building was organised symmetrically around a central axis. Through this symmetry, the reading room obtains a counterpart. For the purpose of its construction, architectural techniques were used to design a room of books and their readers, a room whose identity is tied to the significance of past libraries. As a complement to the introverted, central reading room, flexible and expandable reading islands have been arranged along the library façade.

The façade subtly reveal the function of the building behind them through varying openings in the stone body of the structure. The distances between the pilasters in the façade, which are determined by the ground plan and vary by as much as 1.5 metres (and can also be understood as the spines of books), have an internal connection with the functions of the open stacks and reading areas. The façade was erected using yellow-veined Treuchtlingen marble which makes a strong impression through its natural stone structure, emphasized by a high-pressure water treatment. In the interior decor, calmness and clarity are achieved by reducing the colour palette to just a few tones: white-gray, black-gray, reddish wood (black cherry), dark red and dark green surfaces. The open stacks have been built using glossy black linoleum floors, matte black-grey steel shelves and walls and ceilings painted white.

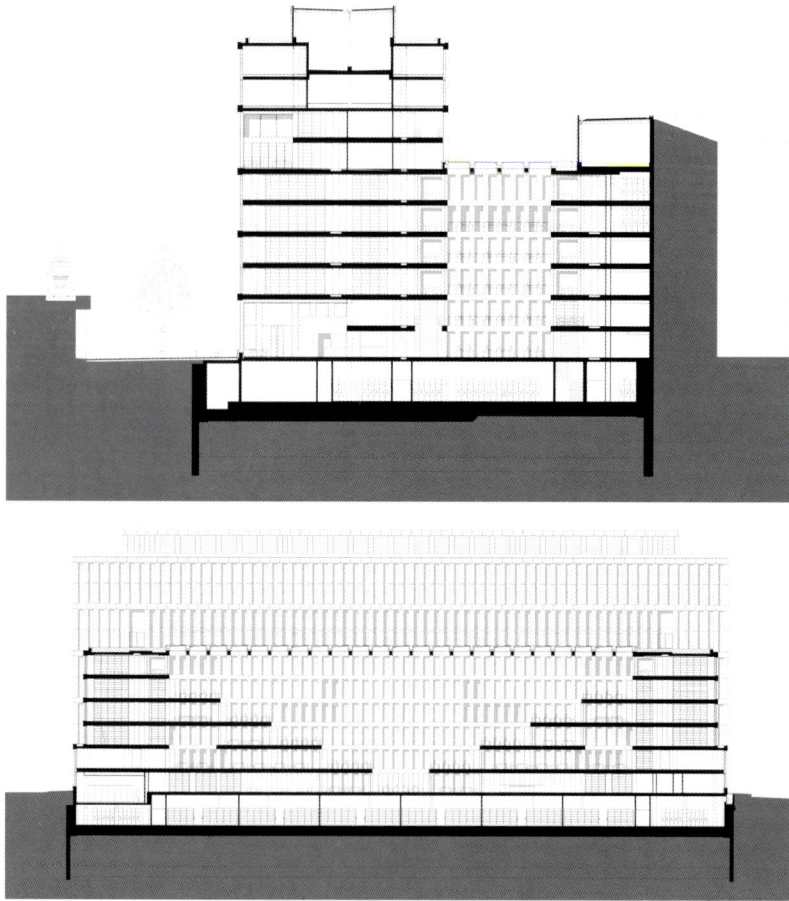

1. View from Japanese Commercial Centre
2. View from southeast

1

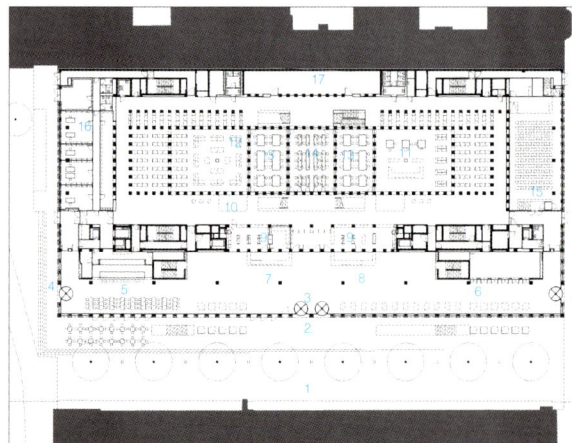

1. Courtyard
2. Main entrance
3. Foyer
4. Side door
5. Cafeteria
6. Information terminal
7. Information desk
8. Return
9. Lending services
10. Self-issue machine
11. Information department
12. Lounge
13. Search
14. Reading room
15. Auditory
16. Administration
17. Print shop
18. Periodicals reading area
19. Workstation
20. PC training
21. PC Pool
22. Video conference
23. Multimedia
24. Copy service

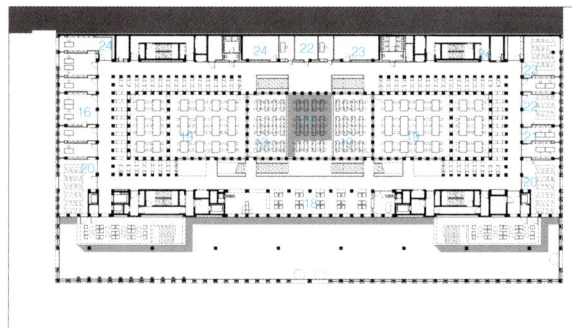

1. Reading terrace with view in the open access area
2. Central Reading Room (with reading terraces)

1. Reading terrace with view in the open access area
2, 3. Central Reading Room (with reading terraces)
4. Carrel details

Ann Arbor District Library – Traverwood Branch

Location: Ann Arbor, USA **Designed by:** inFORM Studio **Completion Date:** 2008 **Photos©:** inFORM Studio **Area:** 1,542 sqm

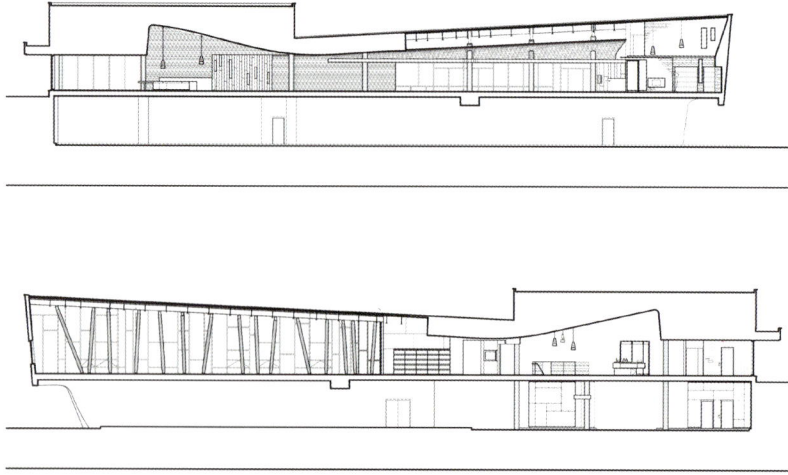

In 2005, the Ann Arbor District Library (AADL) purchased approximately 4 acres of property for a new branch library to serve the northeast quadrant of the city of Ann Arbor. This was to be the third branch library constructed by the current administration since 2002 and would replace a 371.6 square metres branch library within an existing strip mall located along a nearby commercial corridor. The site, heavily wooded and densely vegetated, is located on the southwest corner of Huron Parkway and Traverwood Drive.

During the early stages of the site planning process, the architect collectively began to discuss and investigate considerations for harvesting wood from the site for re-use in the building. Although densely populated, many of the trees were Ash, suffering the effects of the Emerald Ash Borer (EAB). Preliminary research showed that this particular tree species is especially well-suited to milling, as the insect does not damage the interior portion of the wood. With so much value found in a close, abundant, natural resource, unique uses of the wood in the floors, walls, ceiling and structure of the new branch library were proposed and considered.

The utilisation of the Ash would become a major component to the design of the library interior. Integrated as an interior wrapper, the Ash flows from the main entrance floor and walls into a ceiling condition stretching along the entire eastern interior edge of the building and culminating in an Ash wrapped reading rooms whose primary views are focused westward into the forest. Additionally, large sections of the logs were used as structural columns, accommodating vertical and lateral loading along the large southwest expanse of glass. The bark has been stripped from these log columns exposing the randomised grooves and carvings left by the EAB larvae – creating, what is in essences, a visual and tactile testament to the life and destruction of the Ash tree in Michigan and surrounding area, allowing generations to be exposed to an autopsy report of an extinct species in the region.

1. Façade detail
2. General view of façade from the street
3. Main entrance

1

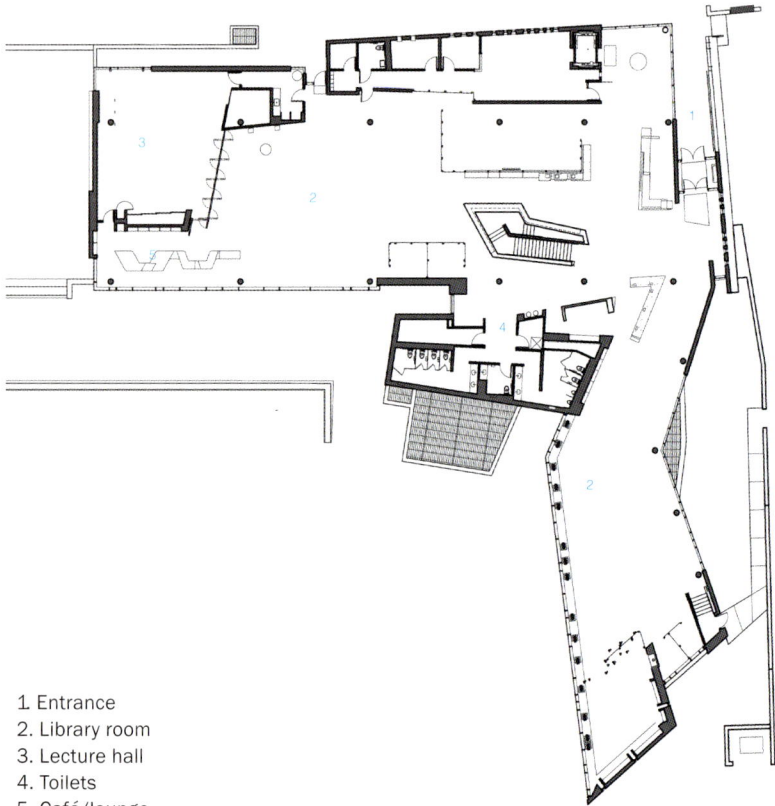

1. Entrance
2. Library room
3. Lecture hall
4. Toilets
5. Café/lounge

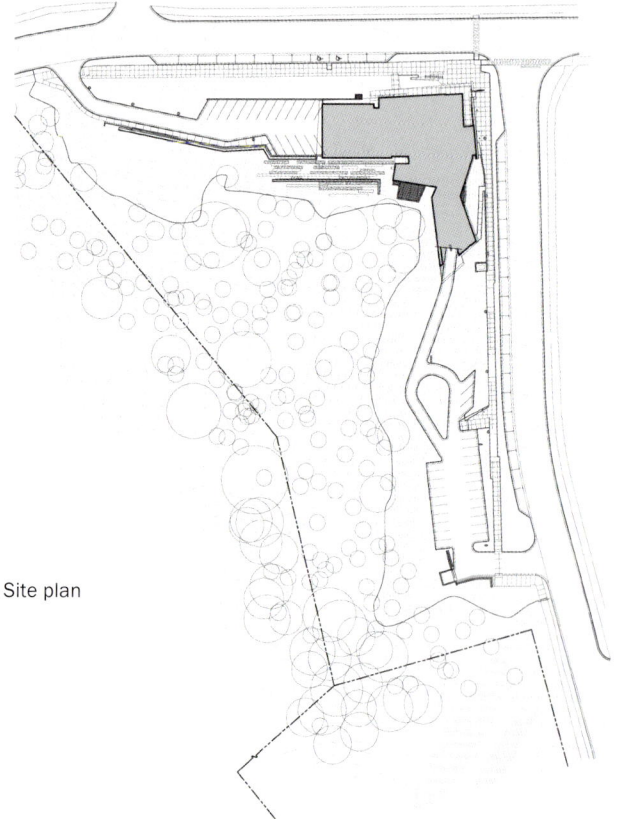

Site plan

1. Entrance to the library interior
2. Lounge
3. Hallway with resting/meeting area

Beth Sholom

Location: San Francisco, USA **Designed by:** Stanley Saitowitz/Natoma Architects **Completion date:** 2008 **Photos©:** Rien van Rijthoven, Bruce Damonte **Awards:** Honour Award, Excellence in Architecture, AIA SF Design Awards, 2009/Best Institutional Building, 46th Annual PCI Design Award, 2008/Best Religious Facilities, California Construction, 2008/High Commendation Award, Religion & Contemplation, World Architecture Festival, 2008/Honour Award, Religious Architecture – New Facilities, Faith & Form Award, 2008/Best Building in San Francisco, Kirby Ward Fitzpatrick Award, 2008

The site is in San Francisco, in the flat Richmond district, at the intersection of Park Presidio and Clement Street. An early plan established a pair of religious structures as gateposts along this boulevard. One is the strong presence of the neo-classical Christian Science Church. The other is Congregation Beth Sholom, where an old synagogue was demolished to build this new building.

A plinth is established. Here all the non-religious programmes of the campus are contained. On the plinth two buildings are placed, forming a courtyard. One is a reflective cube, the social hall, the other a masonry structure, the sanctuary, a vessel floating in air. The origins of this structure are ancient. Solomon's Temple, built in Jerusalem after the Jews returned from exile in Egypt, was a procession of courts, ending with the Holy of Holies.

Here, the entry sequence establishes the distinction of a sacred place in the city through passage. It is a circular journey of turning and rising and turning. The first point of arrival is the lower court from which a stair ascends to the courtyard. Here the three elements of the complex, sanctuary, social hall and existing school are connected. This circular route enables the sanctuary to be entered from the west facing the ark of torahs in the east, an important liturgical requirement.

The design revolves around two key concepts. The essential aspect of Conservative Judaism is that it is egalitarian; women and men participate equally in the liturgy. The Orthodox Jewish Tradition of women separated in a balcony or by a curtain is eliminated. The room is a vessel focussing all worshipers in a single community centred on the Bimah. The other is problem of creating sacred space in the midst of the city. In nature one can sense the power of creation; in the city one is focussed on the works of man. Only the view of the sky presents original nature. The only window in the synagogue is a slice of sky in the ceiling.

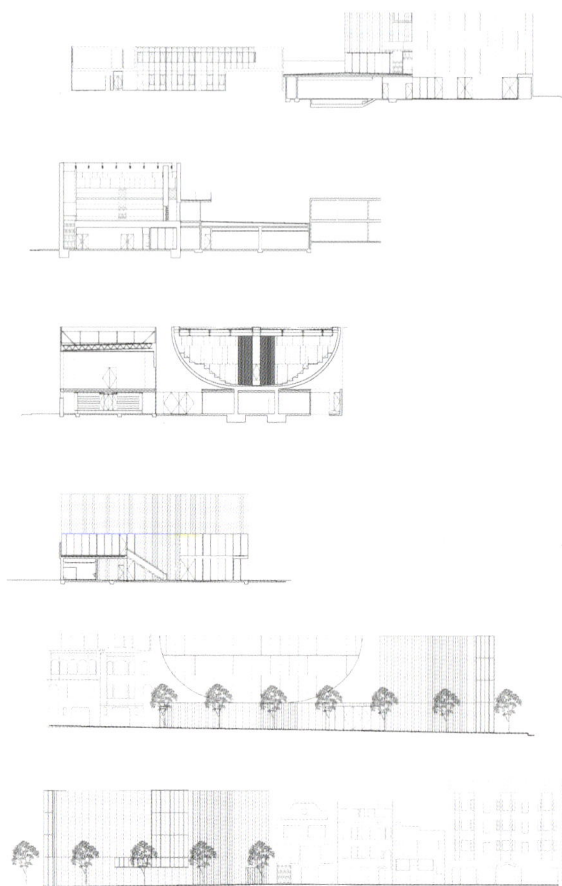

1. General view of front façade
2. Main entrance

1. Back view
2. Side view of front façade
3. Courtyard in the front of entrance

3

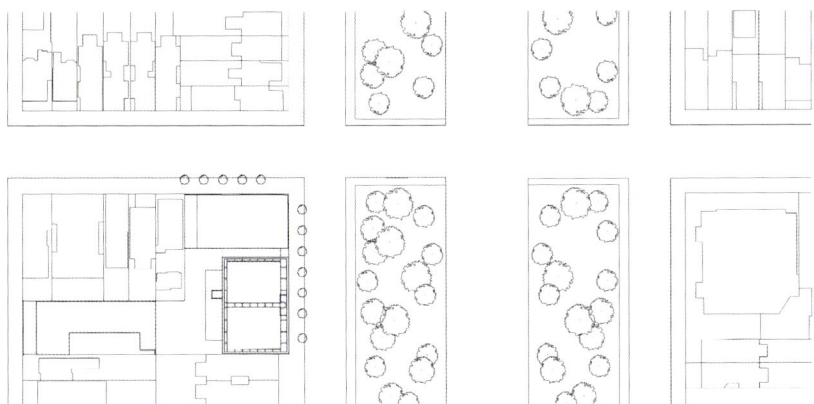

Site plan

4

3

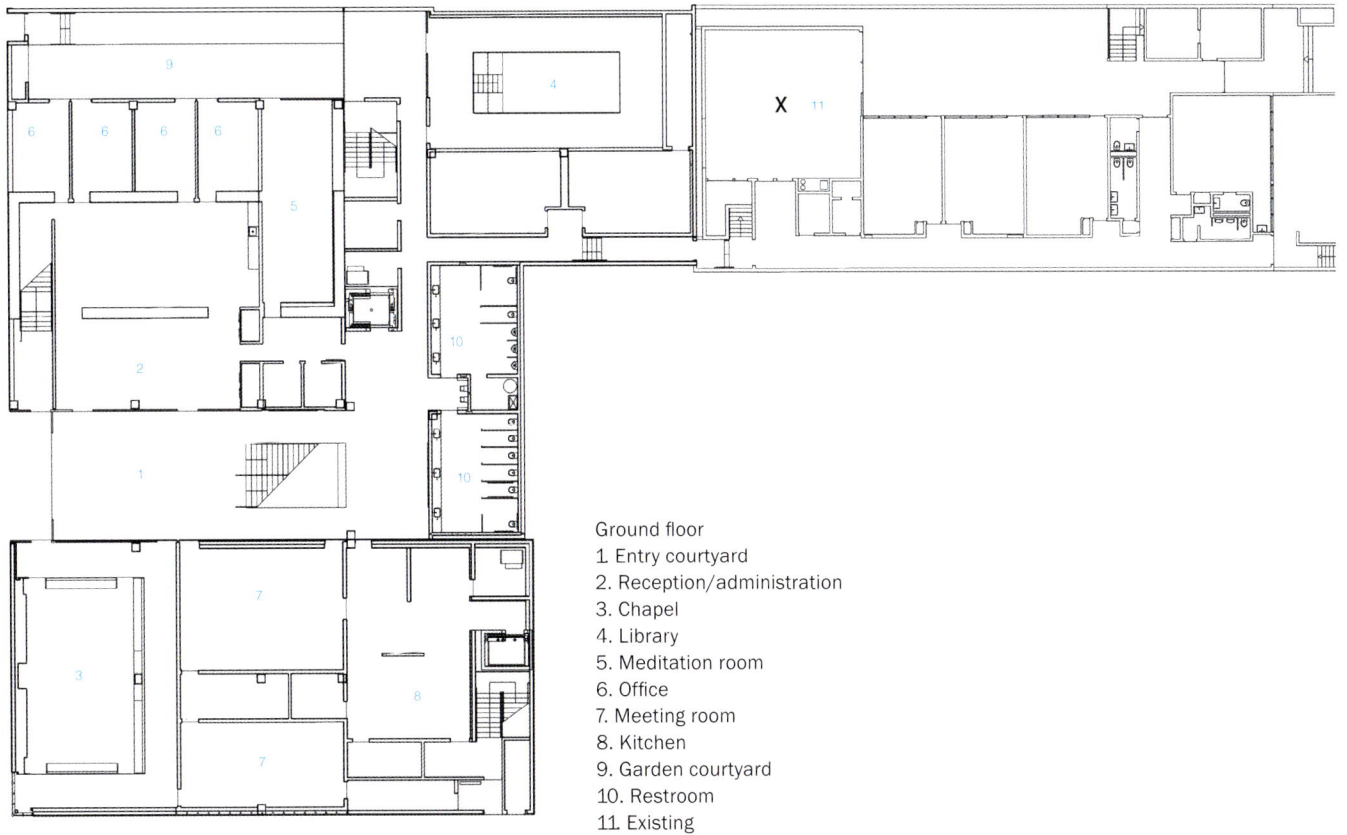

Ground floor
1. Entry courtyard
2. Reception/administration
3. Chapel
4. Library
5. Meditation room
6. Office
7. Meeting room
8. Kitchen
9. Garden courtyard
10. Restroom
11. Existing

1

2

1. Praying room
2. Hallway
3. Intimate spaces
4. View from atrium

3

1-3. Social hall

Kupferberg Holocaust Resource Centre and Archives

Location: New York, USA **Designed by:** TEK Architects **Completion date:** 2009 **Photos©:** Brian Rose Photography **Area:** 2,003 sqm

Located on the campus of Queensborough Community College in Queens, New York, the Harriet and Kenneth Kupferberg Holocaust Resource Centre and Archive consists of the renovation of a former print shop and loading dock in the campus Administration building, and an addition on the south edge of the site. The project provides a much needed home for the Centre, which was previously housed in the basement of the college library, and includes classrooms, work stations, offices, gallery spaces, and a library.

The main interior space of the addition is a gallery that can be reconfigured to accommodate receptions of up to 100 people. A custom steel storefront system containing a variety of glazing types encloses this space and creates contrasting levels of opacity within the different elevations. In addition, the mullions themselves take on contrasting geometries with the regular orthogonal grid of the majority of the volume providing the background for the angled and irregular pattern found on the eastern side. This glazed volume slides out from under a zinc panelled roof, which wraps around the back of the gallery to bracket the two entrances to the building and provide a backdrop to the centerpiece of the project, the exterior terrace.

Clad in Jerusalem Stone, the terrace takes advantage of the existing hilly topography of the site to provide a dramatic vantage point from which to view the main entrance to the campus. The skewed lines and irregular divisions of the steel storefront are a graphic reference to the shattered windows of the Kristallnacht, an anti-Semitic pogrom that occurred in Germany and Austria in November of 1938 in which hundreds of synagogues were destroyed, thousands of homes and businesses were ransacked, and 30,000 Jews were interned in concentration camps. This symbolism relates directly to the primary goal of the centre, which is to provide programmes and resources to educate present and future generations about the ramifications of prejudice, racism and anti-Semitism, and to encourage an awareness of the value of diversity in a pluralistic society.

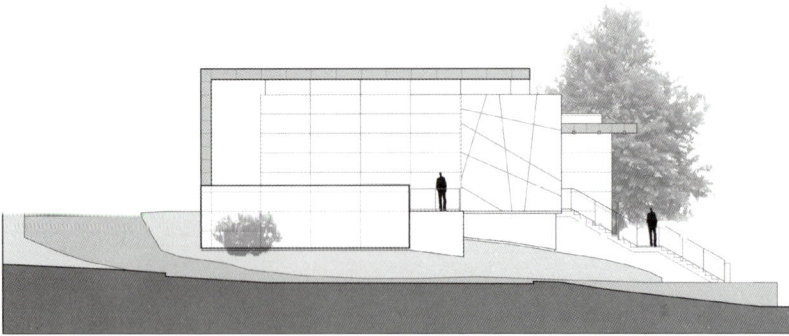

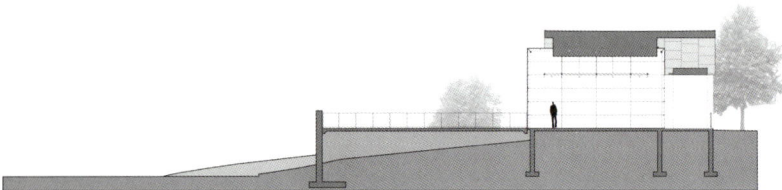

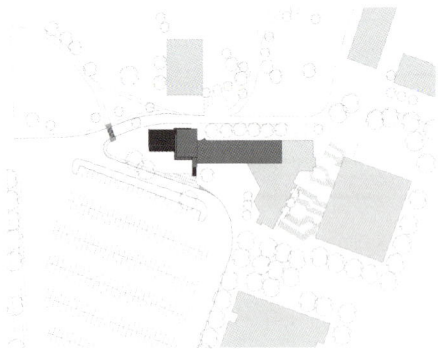

1. Façade detail
2. East entrance, twilight view
3. Entrance

2

1. Side entrance view
2. Front entrance view
3. Exhibition entrance

3

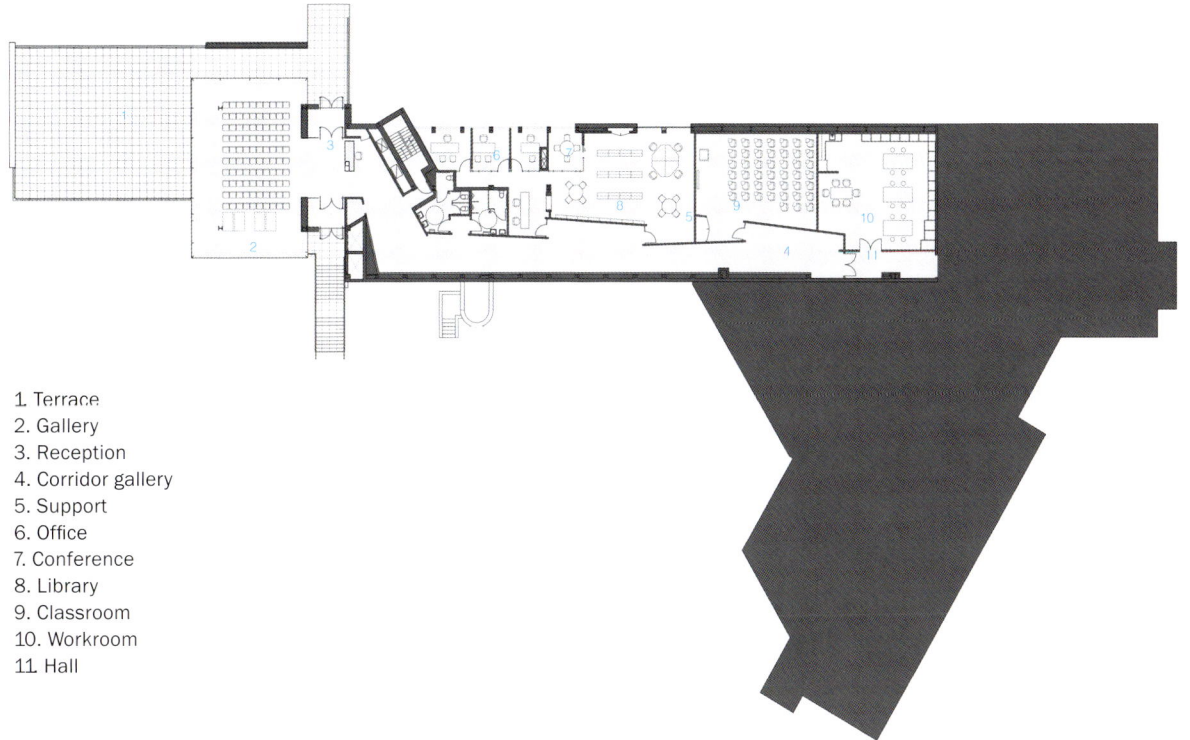

1. Terrace
2. Gallery
3. Reception
4. Corridor gallery
5. Support
6. Office
7. Conference
8. Library
9. Classroom
10. Workroom
11. Hall

1. Alternate exhibit
2. Reception desk
3. Interior exhibit

Peres Centre for Peace

Location: Tel Aviv, Israel **Designed by:** Fuksas **Completion date:** 2008 **Photos©:** Fuksas **Area:** 7,000 sqm

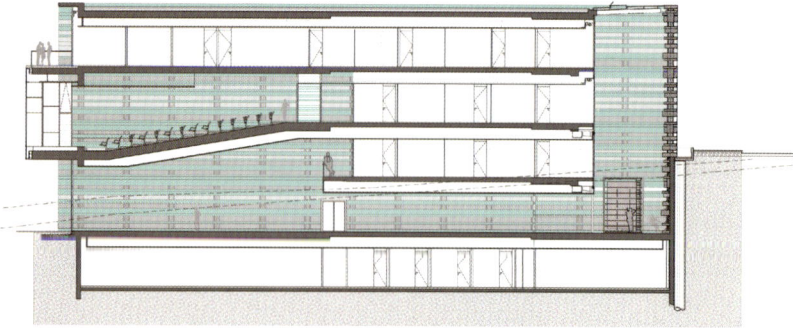

It is a home port for all sailors and a haven for the shipwrecked, to imagine a place that is not virtual, but real. To be dedicated to peace is an immensely taxing undertaking of profound ethical significance.

The outside of the building has alternate layers of concrete and translucent glass. The transparency of the glass will filter the light through to the inside during the day, and by night will send it back outside, entrusting this magical image with the spiritual and concrete message the site will inspire.

The Peres Centre for Peace is a parallelepiped. Obtained by irregularly shaped glass and concrete layers standing on a monolithic base: at one end of the building is the entrance to the car park, and at the other is the pedestrians entrance. At this point the basement becomes a large plaza, an empty space dissected lengthwise by two symmetrical ramps leading inside. This dark and low-ceilinged area leads to the inside of the well of light that is open for the whole height of the building, where the reception area is situated. From here the alternating light and dark layers are visible; the former, in glass, lit from the outside and the latter, in concrete mixed with other materials and local earth. The rest of this floor (total 550 square metres) is designed to house the reception area and exhibition hall.

The remaining six floors, each covering a space of 600 square metres and a height of 3.4 metres. Housing on the ground one are office facilities, a library and cafeteria; on the first floor there is an auditorium to seat 200 people (with a height of 7 metres), the press room and the press conference hall; the members and guest cafeteria is on the second floor with the library; the third and fourth floors house offices and meeting rooms, and the fifth contains ten apartments.

1. Exterior stairs along the building
2. Sea view through glass curtain wall
3. The large plaza connecting with pedestrians entrance
4. Façade detail and distant view of the plaza

3

1 Interior wall detail
2, 3. Staircase and hall way
4. Foyer

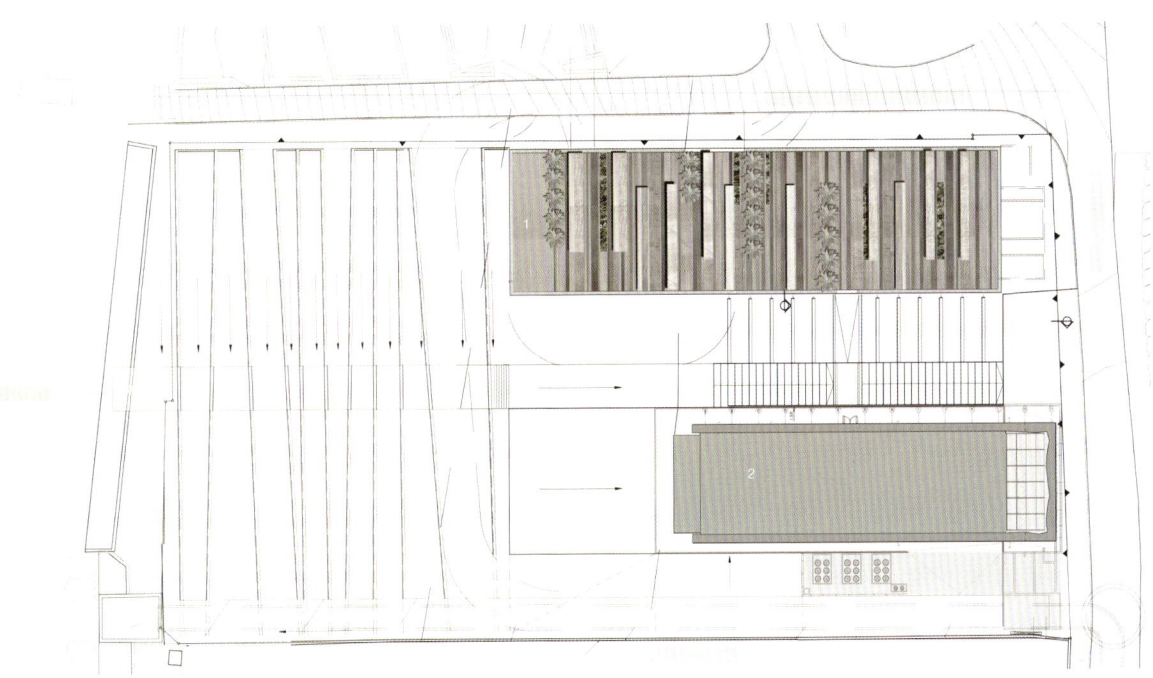

1. Plaza for pedestrians
2. The centre's building

1 Staircase
2. Sea view through window
3. Interior wall detail

3

Danfoss Universe

Location: Nordborg, Denmark **Designed by:** J. MAYER H. **Completion date:** 2007 **Photos©:** J. MAYER H.
Award: The Best Renovations of 2007

The new buildings rise up from the ground and provide spaces that articulate the fusion of outdoor landscape and indoor exhibition. This active ground modulates according to programme and location in the park. The endpoints of the buildings blur the line between building and park by offering inside-out spaces as display areas and projection surfaces related to the temporary exhibitions inside. Silhouettes, as groups of land formations, define the unique newly programmed horizon line of Danfoss Universe.

Danfoss Universe is a science park in Denmark, embedded in the agricultural landscape of Nordborg next to the founder's home and the Danfoss HQ. It opened in May 2005 and is already enlarging due to its considerable success. The master plan for Danfoss Universe Phase 2 includes an exhibition building (Curiosity Centre) and a restaurant (Food Factory), which extends the summer based outdoor park into the winter months by enclosing spaces for exhibitions and scientific experiments.

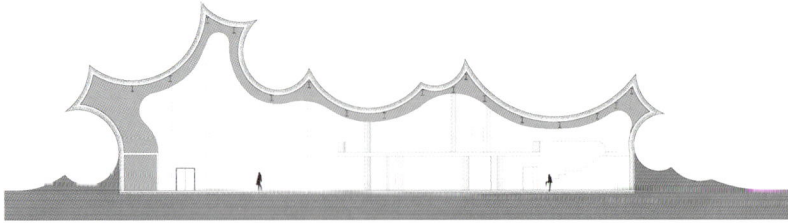

1,2. General view of front façade
3. Side view

1

2

3

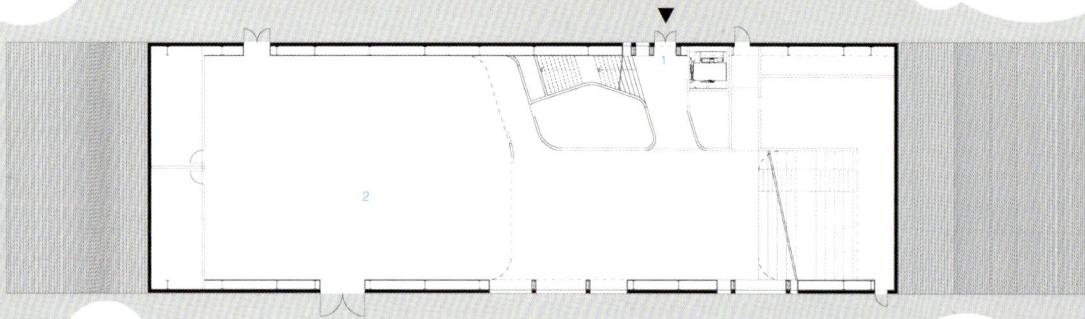

1. Entrance
2. Exhibition space

1. Side view
2. Front plaza
3. Interior activity room

Olympic House and Park

Location: Nicosia, Cyprus **Designed by:** Armon Choros Architektonikis **Completion date:** 2006 **Photos©:** Christos Papantoniou **Awards:** 2009 World Architecture Community Awards, 2007 Selected Work Government of Cyprus Awards, 2007 Proposal Work Mies Van der Rohe Awards, 1999 the 1st Price Architecture Competition for the Olympic House and Park in Nicosia

It was felt that the shifts from "individual to collective" and from "ancient to modern" could be achieved by means of architectural transitions deployed in space, and thus be translated, through mediating voids, into the layout of the building in plan, and its dialogue with the ground in section respectively. On master plan the concord of body and spirit was reflected in the concord of built and non-built, of edifice and park.

With respect to the plan the quest for a layout that would express the global parameter led to the image of an ancient stadium. The building is developed perimetrically around a central void, which opens out to the town, calling upon the "external" to enter and allowing the "internal" to be viewed.

In section, the transition from "ancient to modern" is realised through raising the building high and creating a ground-floor void, where the promenade takes on the significance of museum space for showcasing the ancient and modern history of the institution.

At the master plan level, the building is not juxtaposed to the park, but neither is the reverse true. Initially the built penetrates the un-built part of the plot centrally letting the un-built surround it, while subsequently the un-built penetrates the build centrally and by piercing it, this is incorporated into it. This interpenetration and co-existence of built and un-built, of edifice and park, on an equal footing, expresses the need for material and spiritual to coexist: training for "body and spirit".

The central void, a large space for gatherings, is developed sequentially from the park through the shaded atrium to the entrance lobby and then through the multi-purpose hall once again towards the park. Circulation in the offices is carried out externally so that the spaces be aligned on either side of the atria, just like spectators and, also, of the events taking place within them.

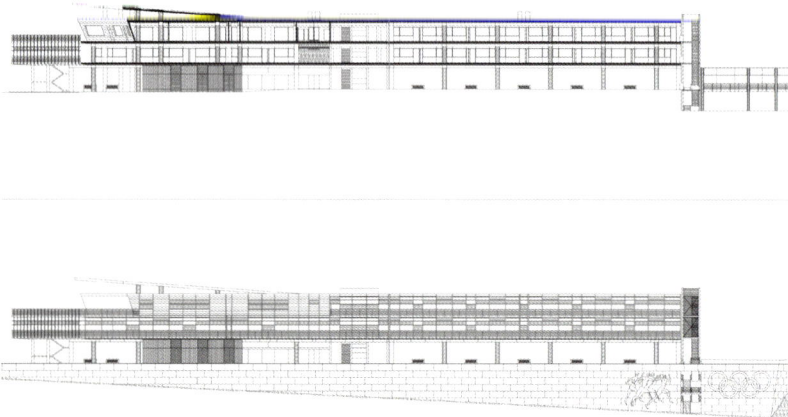

1. General view at night
2. Side view
3. View from the street

2

3

1. View from the parking lot
2. View from the upper terrace
3. Night view detail

3

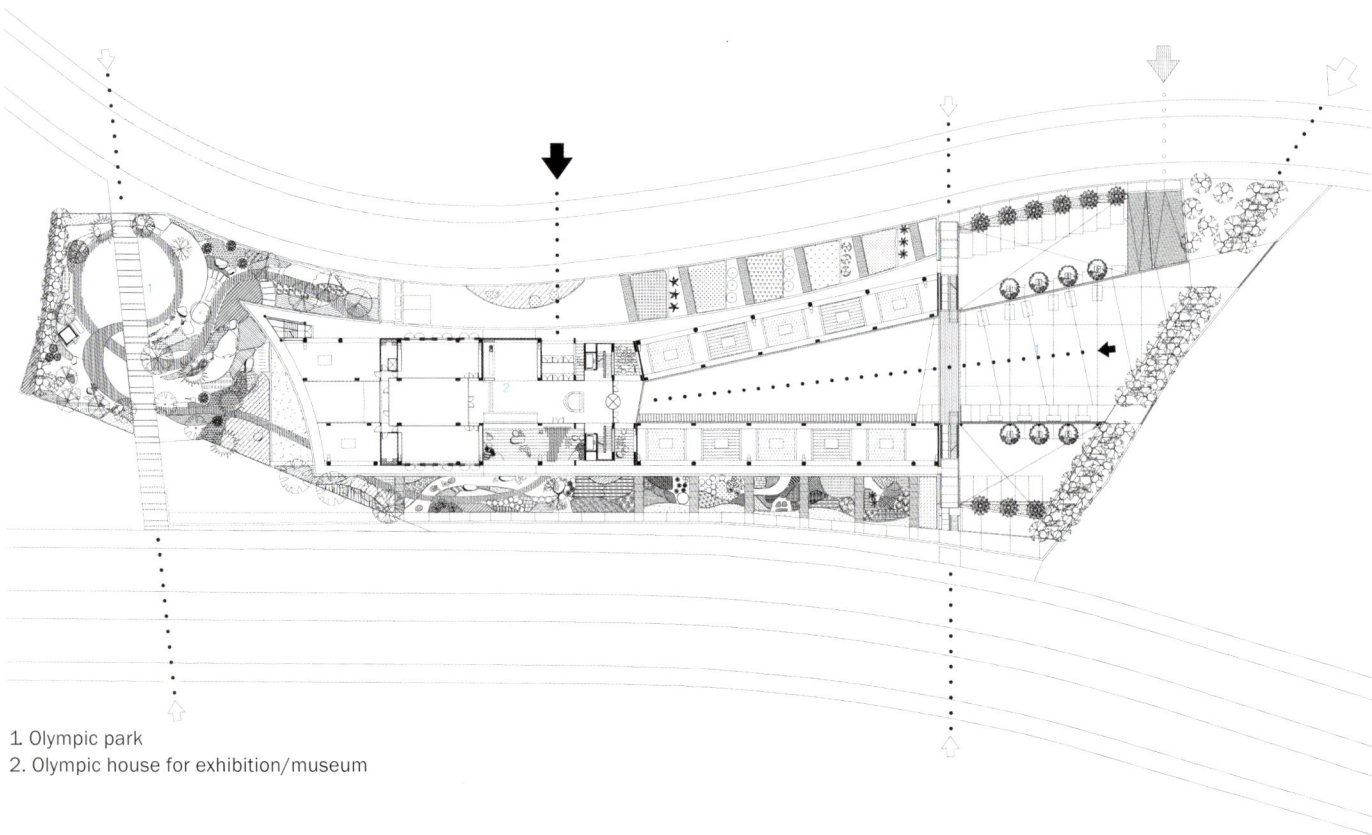

1. Olympic park
2. Olympic house for exhibition/museum

1. Interior exercise yard
2. Sport theme installation
3. Hallway detail

1. Reception
2. Lecture hall
3. Corridor

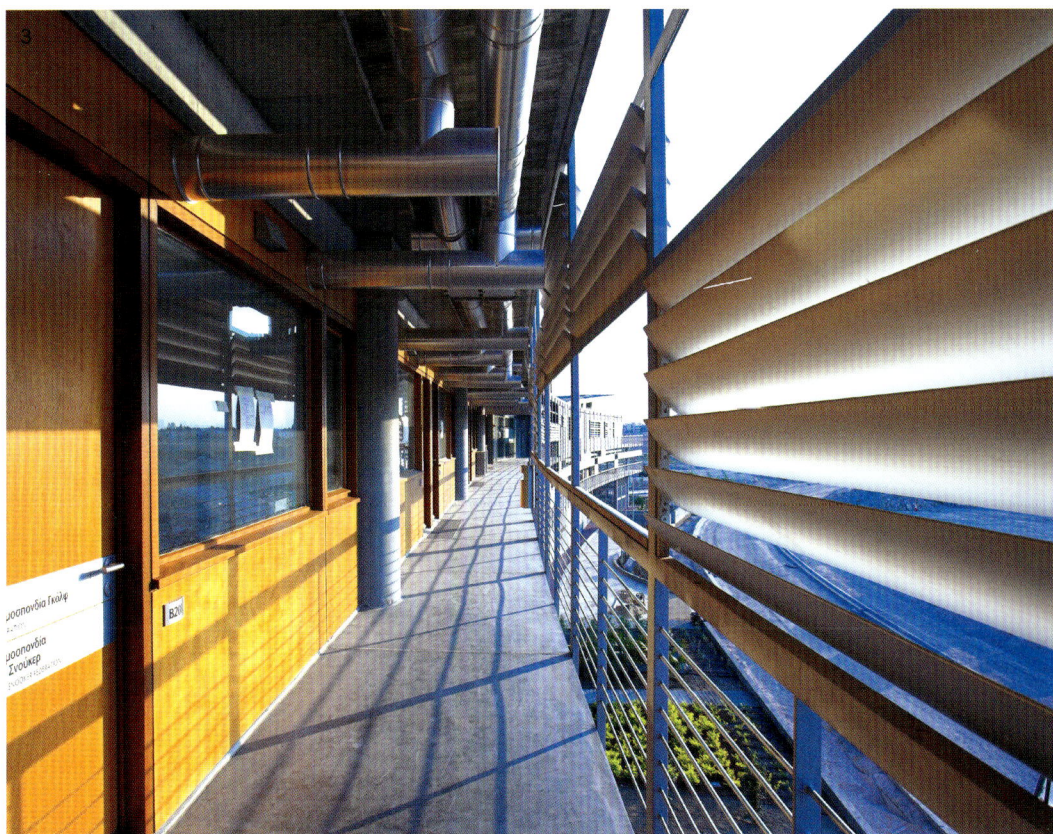

Mora River Aquarium

Location: Mora, Portugal **Designed by:** Promontorio Architects **Completion date:** 2006 **Photos©:** Sérgio Guerra, Fernando Guerra **Awards:** VI Biau Work Award/Award for Best Architectural Work in Ibero-America, built between 2004-2006/2nd Prize, VI Bienal Iberoamericana de Arquitectura y Urbanismo, 2008

The River Aquarium is located in Mora, a small municipality in the Northern Alentejo region. Given the need to shift regional development from the dependence of an increasingly weaker agriculture economy into the environmental tourism and leisure market, the municipality launched a design-and-build competition for an aquarium that could somehow embody the paradigms of biodiversity of the Iberian River.

The plot's gently undulating topography forms a basin at the confluence of two small watercourses. Placing the aquarium at the edge of this quasi-natural retaining lake brought together the fundamental relation between its thematic contents and the presence of fresh water.

The outdoor void between these programme boxes and the pitched shed generate not only accelerated viewpoints onto the outside but also a promenade that culminates in the passage through a bridge over the lake which, in itself, is also a live exhibit of animals and plants collected and nurtured in the region.

The live exhibits, the main feature of an aquarium, reproduce, through complex life support systems, the habitat conditions of different regions allowing to exhibit side-by-side the various animals and plants. On the basement, these support systems guaranty stability of water temperature, PH, quality control and filtering for each habitat parameter, including a duct gallery below each exhibit to supply and monitor the water. For this building, the water is taken from a well on the plot, pumped into a deposit and regenerated after use. In addition, areas for animal quarantine, food preparation, laboratories, staff facilities, and logistics complete the technical floor. Other than the in-situ concrete cast plinth and the white pre-cast porticoes, the programme boxes are built in polished finish plastered terracotta masonry with steel frames and varnished MDF carpentry.

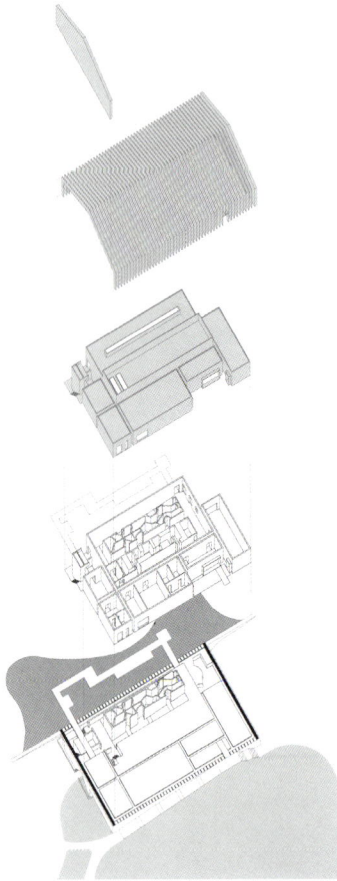

1. Surrounding landscape
2. East façade, viewed over the park
3. West façade

1

2

3

2

3

1. Walkway/ entrance
2. Pitched shelter
3. Façade detail

1. Patio breaking to aquarium
2. Ticket office / store
3. Exhibition entrance
4. Other exhibition
5. Iberian River exhibition
6. Scenic walkway
7. Temporary exhibition room
8. Library / museum
9. Office area
10. Classroom / laboratory
11. Auditorium
12. Auditorium hall
13. Detail tanks
14. Multimedia exhibition
15. First-aid room
16. Cafeteria
17. Kitchen
18. Restaurant

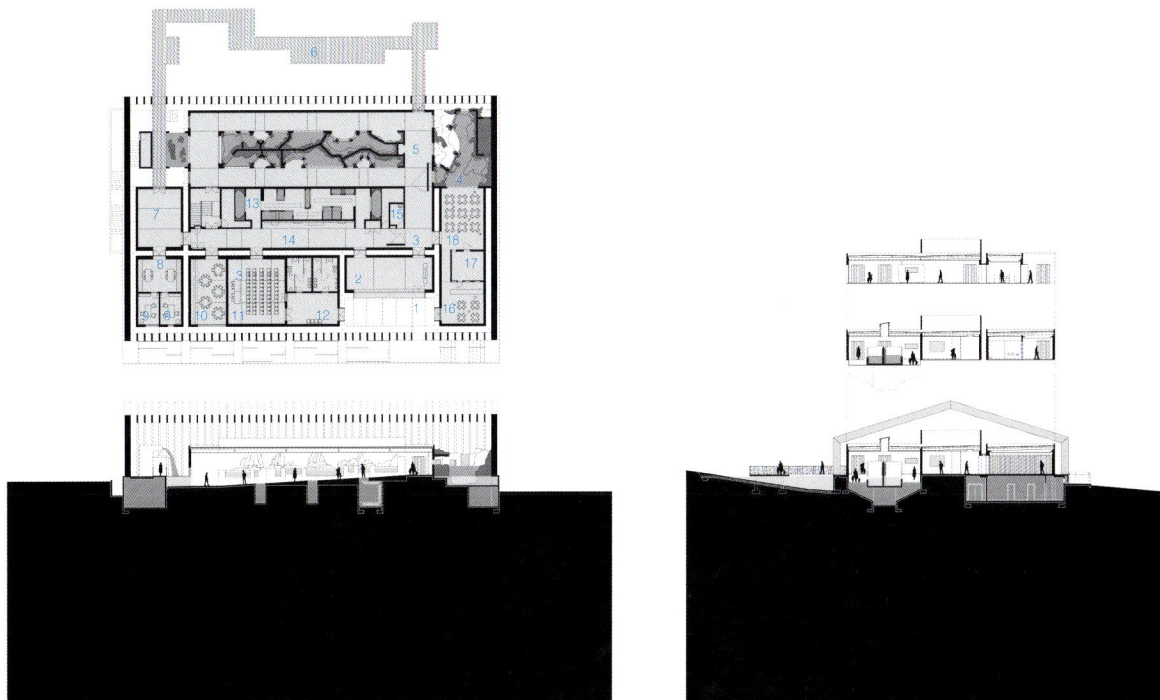

1 Entrance lobby bathing in the sunlight
2. Exhibit room

Aquarium Of San Sebastian

Location: Donostia-San Sebastián, Spain **Designed by:** Hoz Fontan Arquitectos **Completion date:** 2009 **Gross floor area:** 6,200 sqm **Photos©:** José Hevia (www.josehevia.es)

The Aquarium of San Sebastian has been lodged for more than 100 years in a building on Mount Urgull's feet, in one of the most visible zones of La Concha Bay. It is an institution for which its own building, while being at the same time its identity seal, had become an obstacle for its progress.

Divided in two parts, the built-in facilities in the last years were developed in contiguous spaces to the mount, whereas the exhibition area was located at a building in intense contact with the sea. Despite their inner connection, they were divided by the stairs, which connect the two levels of one of the most important strolls of the city of San Sebastian, the "Paseo Nuevo", which lost integrity when arriving to the surrounding area of the Aquarium, turning into just simple stairs that connected with the port. The facilities acquired in the last years would had to be redefined, the building that shelters the exhibition completely renewed, a public elevator should connect the two levels of the new stroll and a new restaurant would have to be constructed in the present building's cover.

The applied strategy uses the relocation of the programme's peripheral components to optimise the internal functioning of the museistical institution, providing new exhibition space. The restaurant constructed in the present building's cover, guarantees the operativity of the Aquarium during the construction, and at the same time defines a square where the new stroll acts as a viewing-point on La Concha Bay. A public elevator will be part of the colonisation of the lower parts that surround the Aquarium as spaces of transit management, which makes possible a total reframing of the internal circulations of the building, and thus, of the museistical experience.

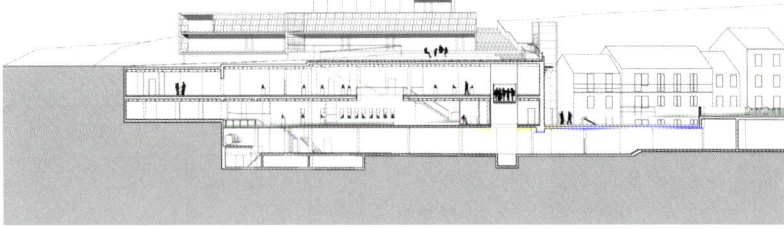

1. New main entrance
2. Ending of the Paseo Nuevo stroll
3. Bokado Restaurant
4. Bokado Restaurant and Jacques Square

3

4

1. Bokado Restaurant
2. Jacques Cousteau Square
3. Back façade

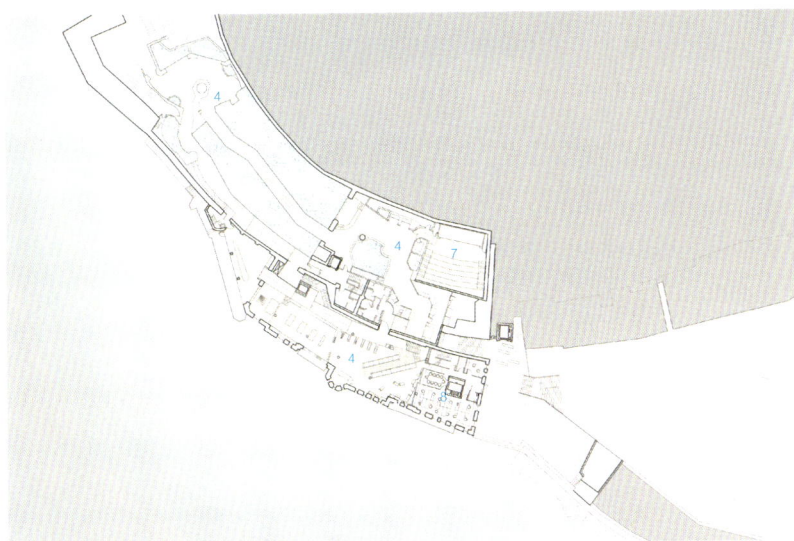

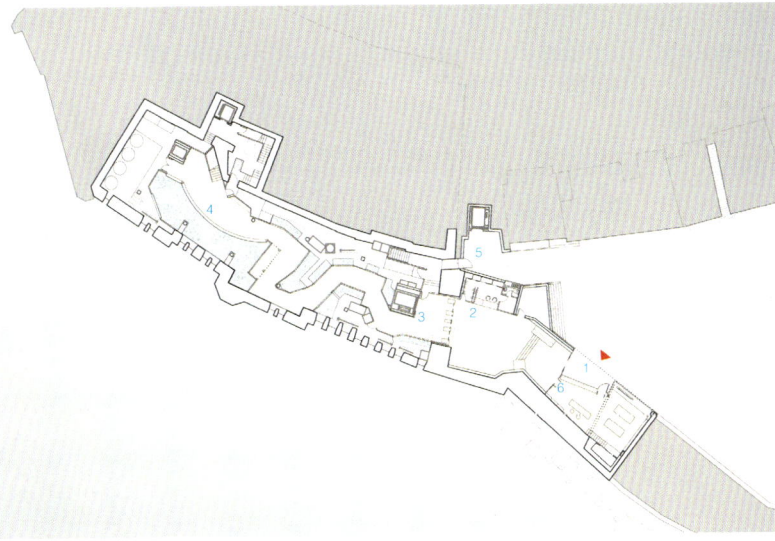

Floor plan

1. Entrance
2. Tickets
3. Elevator
4. Exhibition space
5. Public elevator
6. Lounge
7. Auditorium
8. Bokado Restaurant

1. Exhibition space
2. Lounge

2

Ibaiondo Civic Centre

Location: Vitoria-Gasteiz, Spain **Designed by:** ACXT Architects-Jesús Armendariz Eguillor, Amaia Los Arcos Larumbe and David Resano Resano **Completion date:** 2009 **Photos©:** Josema Cutillas **Area:** 14,000 sqm

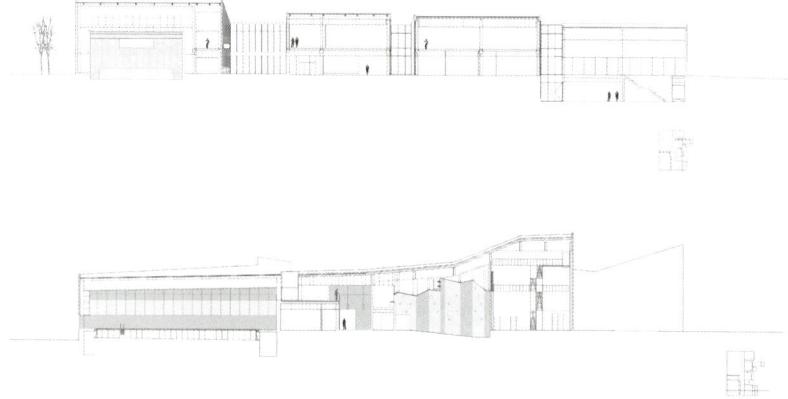

Ibaiondo Civic Centre has a 14,000 square metres area and is located in Vitoria-Gasteiz, Spain. Sport, leisure and administrative services for neighbours at different parts of the City are joined together in these types of public buildings.

Once all interior functional, spatial and organisational requirements were defined, the project searched for an extroverted look to appeal the citizens, as to get the perception of the whole building to provide enough information of the public services to be provided there: theatre, leisure and sports swimming pool, solarium, café, indoor sports centre, library, workshops, council citizens help points, etc.

The project avoids forms of an elaborate façade composition, and shows itself as irregular and polyhydric, with a leisure personality. Because of such diversity at interior layouts, the exterior catches the citizen's eye, specially the polymer concrete façades, with a multidirectional groove to create an optical polychromatic illusion.

The building interior layout follows extensive and strict functionality criteria defined by the Council technical team at competition phase. Sport services (swimming pool and indoor sports centre) are located to the north following a "Cartesian" geometry, due to their sizes and scale. So the rest of services are created to the south, with some sort of volumetric anarchy facing the residential area. Other uses are organised along a corridor separating and linking together different services. From this corridor, through glass enclosures, the visitor can recognise the different activities inside the building, as a suggestive "showroom".

Energy sustainability in the building is ratified by a high energy efficiency qualification, obtained by ensuring good thermal isolation and high equipment performances. Also an approximate 700 square metres area of solar thermal collectors provide energy to heat water for both swimming pool and building hot running water. This dedicated design generates an estimated CO_2 emissions saving of up to 1,900 tons.

1. General day view and front plaza
2. Side view
3. General view in dusk

2

3

Ground floor
1. Lobby
2. Control room
3. Showroom
4. Theatre
5. Citizen services
6. Coffee bar
7. Meeting point
8. Youth club
9. Dance room
10. Photography
11. Changing room
12. Indoor pool
13. Machinery
14. Sports court
15. Paddle court
16. Computers
17. Kitchen
18. Ceramic
19. Miscellaneous
20. Toy library

1, 2. Indoor pool
3. Auditorium

1. Gallery
2. Toy library access
3. Corridor

Documentation and Information Centre of Bergen-Belsen Memorial

Location: Hanover, Germany **Designed by:** KSP Jürgen Engel Architekten **Completion:** 2007 **Photos by:** Klemens Ortmeyer **Gross floor area:** 4,849 sqm

The brief to redesign the architecture of the Bergen-Belsen Memorial is a challenging task in terms of subject-matter and, in several respects it is absolutely essential that a sensitive approach be brought to this site of German history.

The Memorial redesign envisages developing the historical site of the camp appropriately, allowing visitors to get a feeling for the camp's former spatial structures. A "stone path" starting on the Memorial's forecourt runs through the new building, leading the visitor on from the Memorial area into the actual former site of the camp. This path is the element integrating the outside complex with the architecture.

The main body of the long documentation centre building made of exposed concrete lies in a corridor through the now thick forest. This corridor follows the original path of the country road from Walle to Hörsten. The new building lies outside the former concentration camp, extending hesitantly only a couple of metres beyond the boundary of the former camp.

This act of guiding visitors along a spatially demarcated and staged outdoor path is mirrored inside the building. A path/space continuum is overlain by the changing volumes of the interior rooms. Changes of direction, the sequence of different room volumes, accompanied by a few specific insights into the otherwise closed body of the building are all aimed at distancing the visitor from his everyday world.

The tour leads from the two-storey half-some of the "mood-setting area", past various theme-related exhibitions on the prisoner-of-war and concentration camp to the long and slightly upward-sloping large exhibition hall. The end of this hall is at the same time the turning point on the tour and serves to provide "historic/topographical information". This is the area which overlaps with the site of the former camp. A large through-cut in the body of the building allows visitors to survey the outside, thus incorporating the site of the former camp into the exhibition. The path continues through the exhibition on the upper storey, allowing views backward into the big hall, the vestibule and out into the "stone bridge" outdoor area.

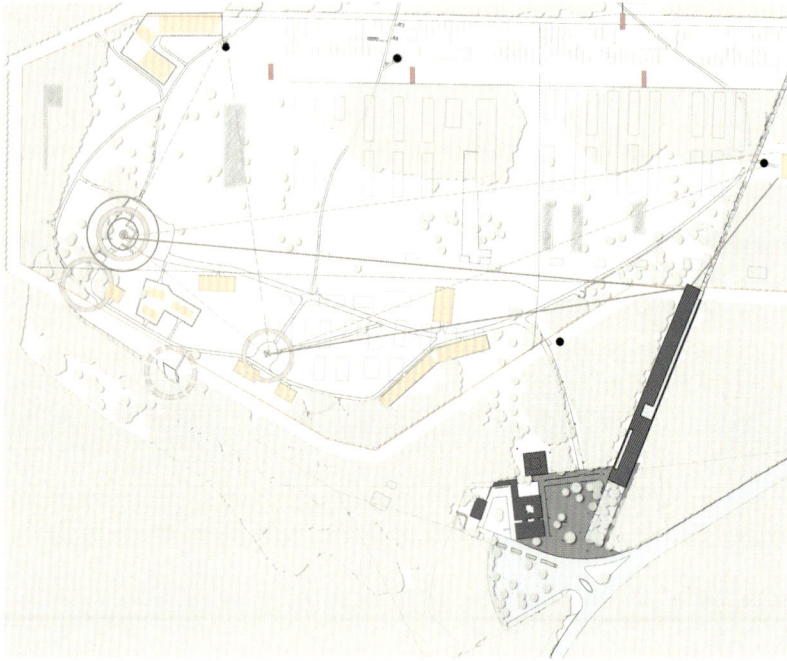

Masterplan

1. Corridor
2. Façade detail
3. Exterior dusk view
4. Façade detail

3

4

3

1-3. Showing area

Floor plan

1. Cafeteria
2. Foyer
3. Bookshop
4. Courtyard
5. Prologue
6. Exhibition "The Wehrmacht Pow Camp"
7. Film tower
8. Stony path
9. Exhibition "The Bergen-Belsen Concentration Camp"
10. Topography

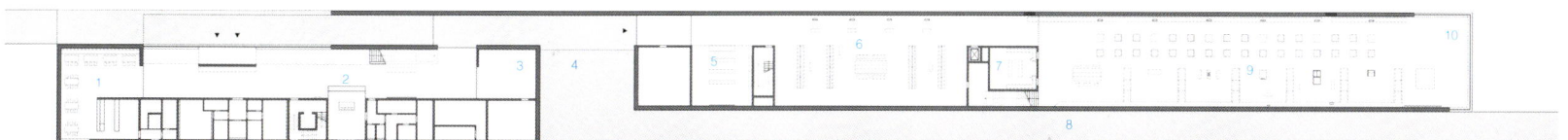

EDF Archives Centre

Location: Bure-Saudron, France **Designed by:** LAN Architecture **Completion date:** 2011 **Photos©:** Julien Lanoo **Construction area:** 6,800 sqm **Awards:** Saie Selection 2010 – 2nd/International Architecture Awards 2009, the Chicago Athenaeum & Museum of Architecture and Design/ INTERARCH 2009 – Special Award from the Architectural Society of Soa/Archi Bau Awards 2009 – 1st price – Green Building

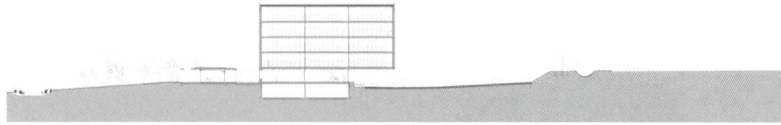

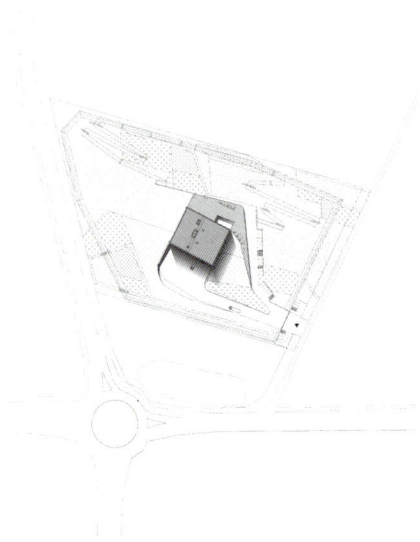

This building, symbol of the long term and visible presence of EDF in the Meuse and Haute Marne region, hosts the company's industrial records. Within the framework of the Meuse and Haute Marne economic support programme, EDF has decided to centralise all its intermediary Engineering Production Management archives in Bure-Saudron.

The new centre allows the documents' organisation and it also ameliorates the storage and the utilisation processes. These archives, on paper-based and microfilm-based formats, will occupy about 70 kilometres of shelves. The building has also a laboratory for micro-films, specifically designed for this purpose.

The architect realised a five-level, 19-metre high building within a plot of 3.3 hectares, and the an archives area covers approximately 1,400 square metres and a total surface of approximately 7,000 square metres.

This approach results in: considerable saving in terms of the building's envelope, a marginal impact on the landscape (with view points at a considerable distance from the building), the possibility of a maximum use of the excavated land around the building's footprint to control water recuperation and treatment on the site, an energetically and environmentally extremely high performance building, the creation of a symbol representative of the approach taken by the Mouse and Haute Marne economic support programme.

To give the impression of a lightweight building in movement, the architect proposed incorporating stainless steel studs into the earth-coloured concrete cladding. This solution had the effect of blurring the building's limits and reflecting the surrounding colours and changing seasons.

The envelope has a very high performance resulting from the materials employed and the technology used for attaching the concrete facing (reduced thermal bridges). The combination of two layers of concrete (structure + facing) and insulation (30 centimetres) ensures that the building has a high level of inertia favouring comfort during the summer and reduces cooling requirements.

1. Surrounding natural landscape viewed from the archive centre
2. Entrance hallway
3, 4. General day view

3

4

1. Meeting room
2. Entrance and corridor
3. Office

3

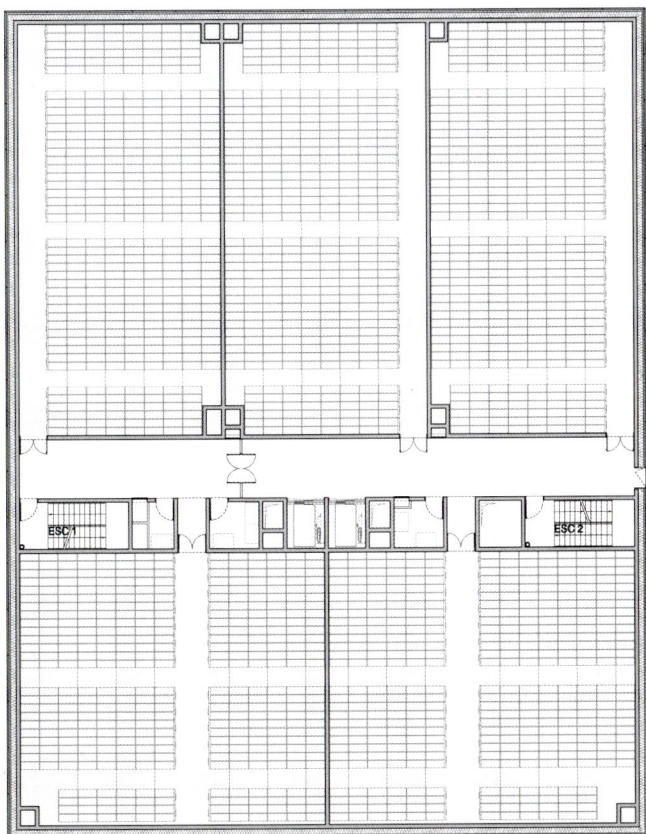

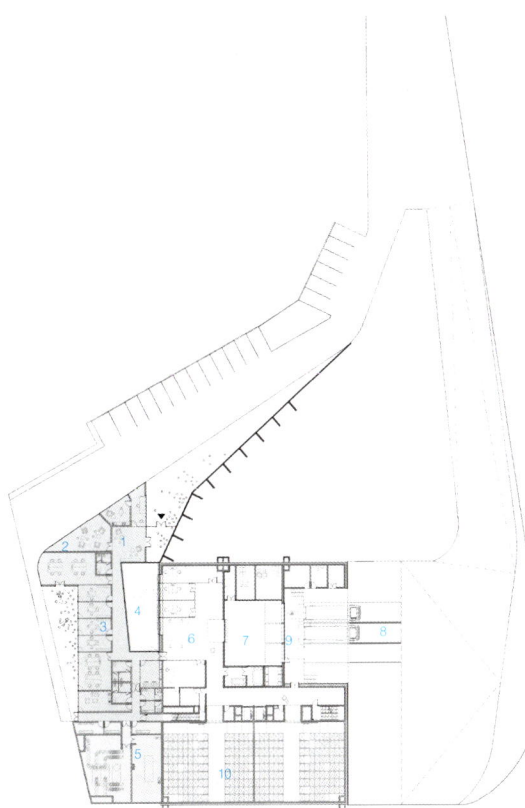

Offices & staff premises
1. Entrance hall
2. Multipurpose hall
3. Offices
4. Patio
Technical premises
5. Technical premises
Logistic and treatment area
6. Sorting area
7. Transit area
8. Delivery area
9. Unloading platform
Archives storage
10. Archives storage

Ars Electronica Centre

Location: Linz, Austria **Designed by:** Treusch Architecture **Completion date:** 2008 **Photos©:** Treusch Architecture **Building area:** 3,336 sqm **Awards:** Nominated for WAF Award (World Architecture Festival), shortlisted under the "Culture" Category/Civic Trust Award 2009: City of Culture Award

Situated between the River Danube and the historic buildings on the one hand and the new Ars Electronica Centre on the other, the open deck of Treusch's extension – the "heart of the Centre" – provides public space and seating for open-air theatre and presentations and seems to be perfectly integrated into the city's events.

The main thought behind the design has been to create a sculptured building with a structure totally accessible by foot, and therefore an exciting experience within itself. The existing Ars Electronica Centre and the new extension are connected to form one unit to be perceived as an ensemble. The crystal-like appearance generates a homogeneous interaction with its surroundings, at the same time becoming a distinctive landmark.

The exhibition area is located beneath this outdoor platform the main deck between the main building and the future lab facilities can be flexibly divided into larger or smaller exhibition areas.

The future lab facilities – for media art research – comprise laboratories and workshops in the basement with offices and recreation rooms above. The upper deck, which is also an outdoor platform two storeys higher than the main deck, offers space for additional exhibition areas, presentations, events, etc.

The existing Ars Electronica Centre is connected to the new main and supply building by a steel & glass construction. The double glass façade, partly transparent and partly translucent, can be illuminated by LED (liquid emitting diode) technology installed in the space between the two layers of the façade. Each façade element with its own LED panel can be individually controlled, with colour and brightness/intensity (RGBW) infinitely variable.

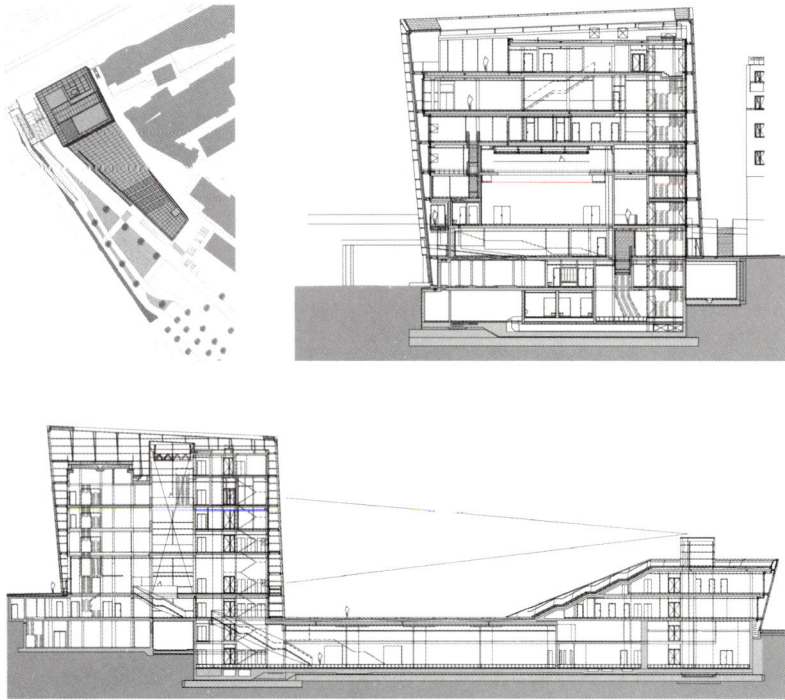

1. General view in dusk
2. Side façade detail

3

1. Front plaza
2. Top view of the plaza and the building
3. Side façade detail

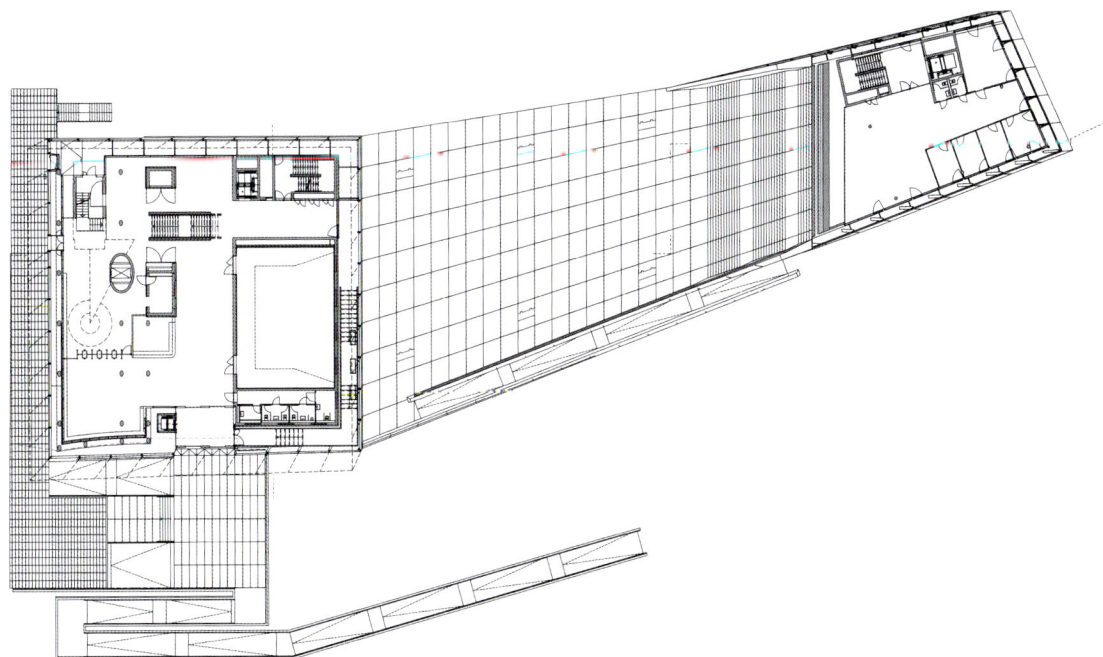

Floor plan

1. Entrance lobby and reception
2. Hallway and lounge area

Nanjing University Performing Arts Centre

Location: Nanjing, China **Designed by:** Preston Scott Cohen **Completion date:** 2009 **Photos©:** Preston Scott Cohen **Construction area:** 16,000 sqm

The Nanjing University Performing Arts Centre, located centrally in the master plan for the new Nanjing University campus in Xianlin, offers a singular expression of the dialogue between two opposed paradigmatic forms of symbolic significance: a curving roof related to the landscape of the larger campus context, and a tower which acts as a beacon and observation point.

The design exploits the techniques and economy of local construction practices as a means to develop an exceptional form. Poured-in-place concrete construction, using adjustable and recyclable form work, gives shape to a landscape-like roof that acts as a unifying "umbrella". The roof form is derived from a series of hyperbolic paraboloids, the ruling lines of which become reinforcing beams, all based on the same cross section, and distributed at regular intervals. As such, the roof creates the effect of a remarkably variable form, despite its underlying logic of regularity and economy of means. The roof landscape surrounds the tower in such a way that it appears as if the tower is an anchored point of resistance or a buoy atop the surface of a roiling seascape.

The interior offers a flowing plan that accommodates a complex series of interrelated programmes of student organisations and spaces for events. The auditorium is the most important space, with seating that establishes a setting conducive to a unique social experience for diverse audiences. The spiraling form of the building is extended by a stair that ascends the outside of the tower. One of two fire stairs is outside the body of the tower, thus allowing the unusually small floor plate that gives the tower its distinctive scale.

The design of the building was driven by an economical and efficient passive energy strategy. By strategically dividing the building into several functionally independent zones, parts of the building that are not in use can be closed off thermally from those parts that are, dramatically reducing heating and cooling loads. Working with fluid dynamics modeling software, the tower's interior organisation and exterior form (a narrow floor plate oriented towards prevailing winds) allow for cross-ventilation satisfying the building's summertime cooling demands.

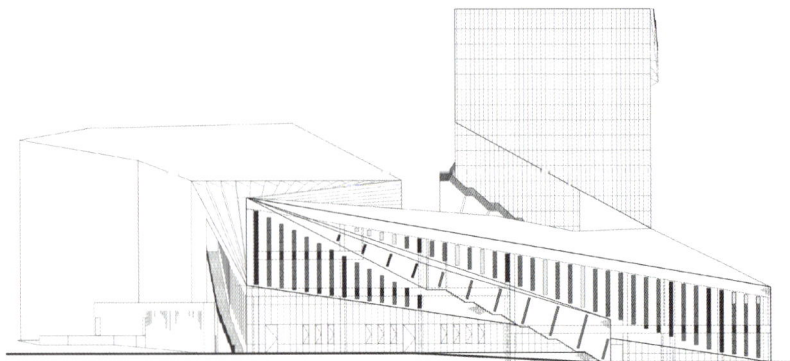

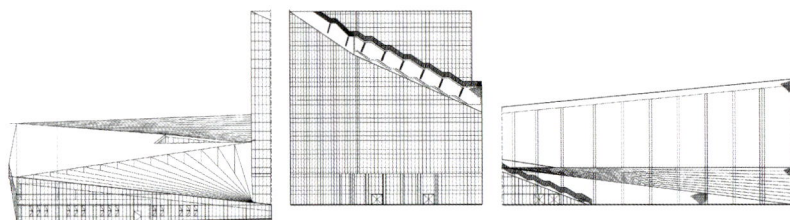

1. North façade
2. Northwest view
3. Tower and east wing

1

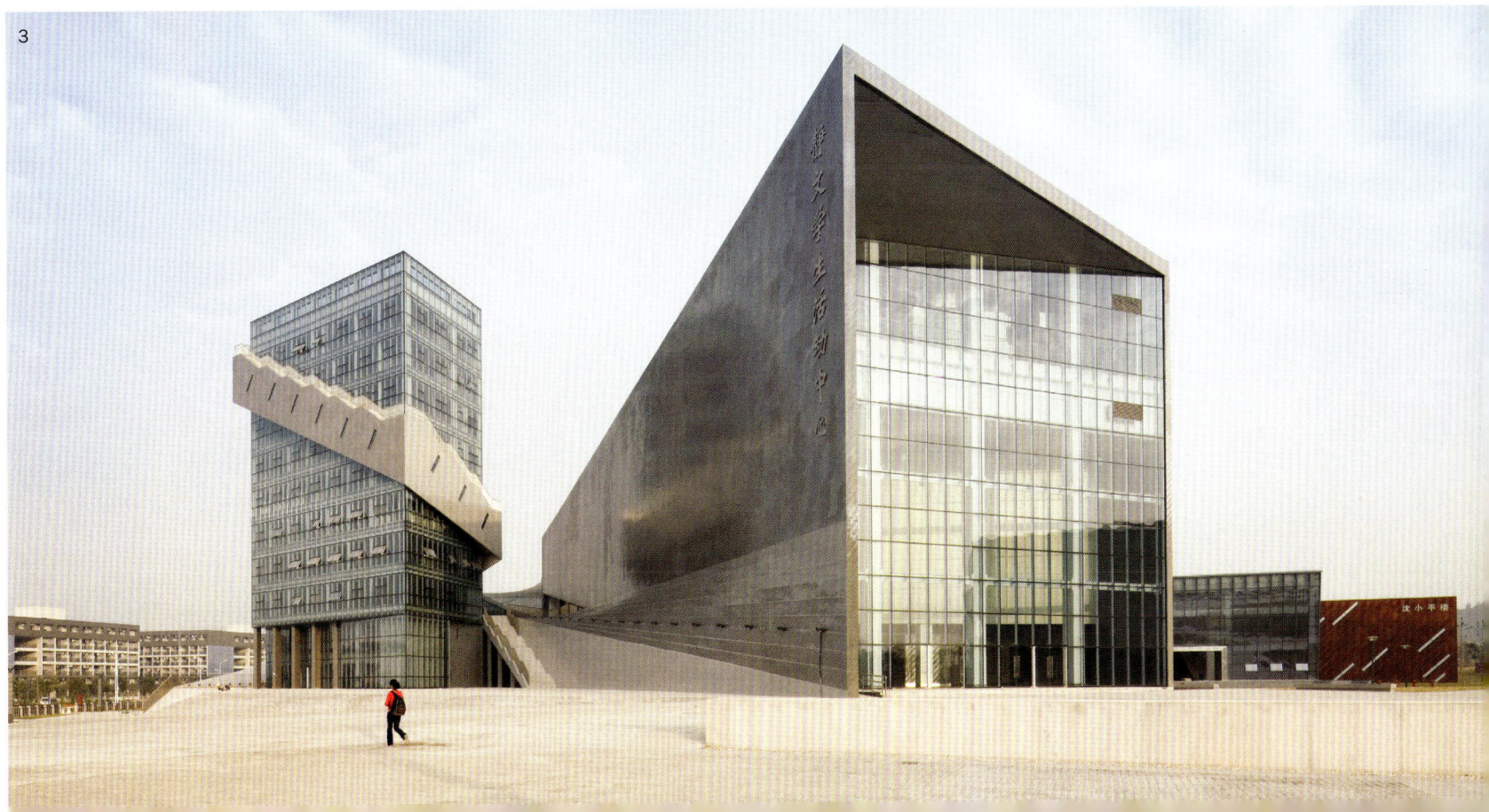

1. Tower and east façade
2. Hall

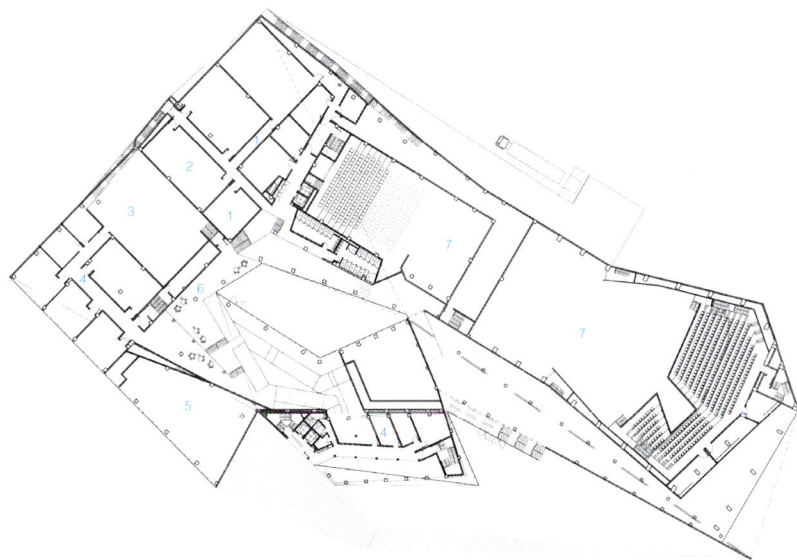

Plan 1
1. Activity room
2. Psychology room
3. Multifunctional hall
4. Radio station
5. Music bar
6. Lounge
7. Auditorium

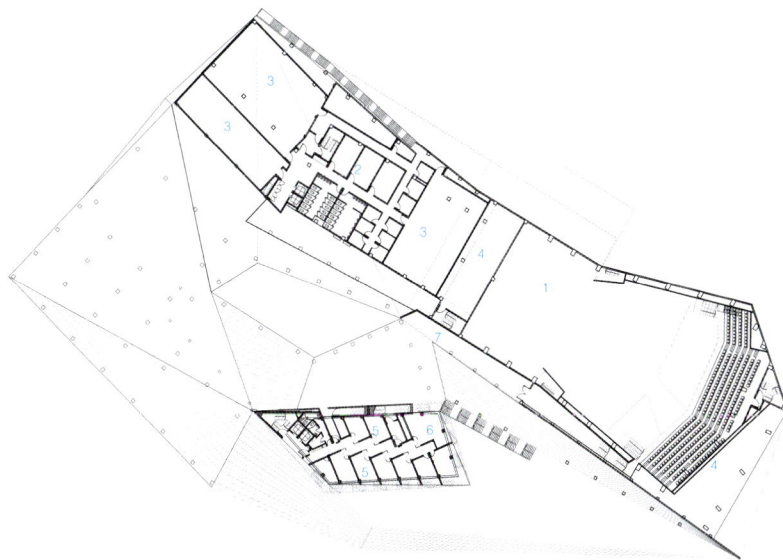

Plan 2
1. Auditorium
2. Practice room
3. Activity room
4. HVAC
5. Office
6. Conference room
7. Lobby

1 Interior atrium
2. Ceiling detail

2

New Art Exchange

Location: Nottingham, England **Designed by:** Hawkins Brown **Completion date:** 2008 **Photos©:** Helene Binet, Tim Crocker **Award:** 2009 RIBA Award

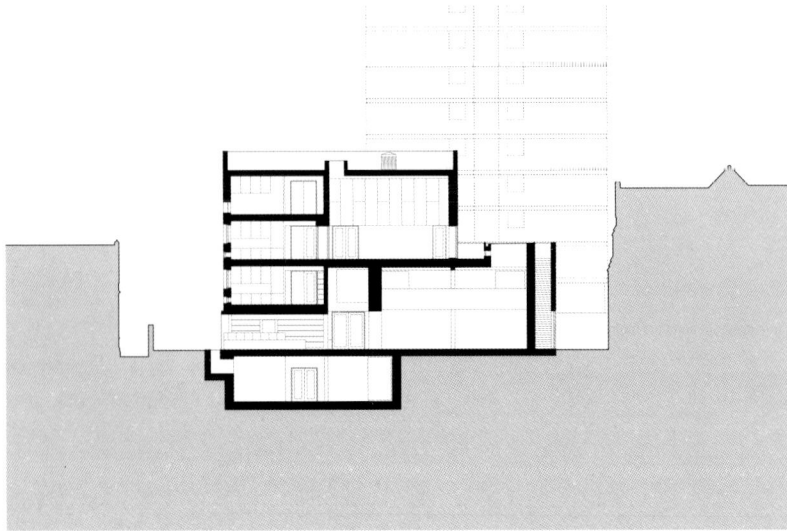

Located on the site of the New Art Exchange's original building, a former dispensary on Gregory Boulevard in Hyson Green in Nottingham, the New Art Exchange provides new facilities for the Hyson Green community, helping to regenerate one of the East Midland's most deprived areas.

The building launches the New Art Exchange as the UK's first regional inner city contemporary visual arts centre led by African, African Caribbean and South Asian artistic practice. Situated within close proximity to Djanogly City Academy, the local library and community centre brings a new social and cultural dimension of the Hyson Green neighbourhood.

The 4-storey building provides 1,360 square-metres floor space, which is divided into a visual arts gallery, workshop spaces, studios, rehearsal spaces and facilities for an artist in-residence. The building, which deploys a concrete frame to support a semi-glazed external skin, is distinguished from the ubiquitous red clay buildings of the neighbourhood by its black brick façade. A playful arrangement of frameless windows ranging in size (from 0.16 square metres to 4.84 square metres) offers incidental and unexpected views into and out of the building.

HawkinsBrown worked directly with visual artist Hew Locke who has made a site-specific ceiling installation in the ground floor café which comprises aluminium plates embossed with imagery of the local area. The installation provides a counterpoint to the building's rigorous rectilinear form as well as celebrating and promoting the centre's relationship with its immediate locality.

1. Entrance viewed from the street
2. The building is finished in a semi-glazed black brick, distinguishing it from the ubiquitous red clay buildings of the neighbourhood

1. The building is flanked by two red clay buildings: the local library and a community centre
2. The natural ventilation of the first floor rehearsal space is also acoustically lined with automated black out blinds to all openings

2

1. Entrance
2. Café
3. Kitchen
4. Lobby
5. Reception
6. Gallery

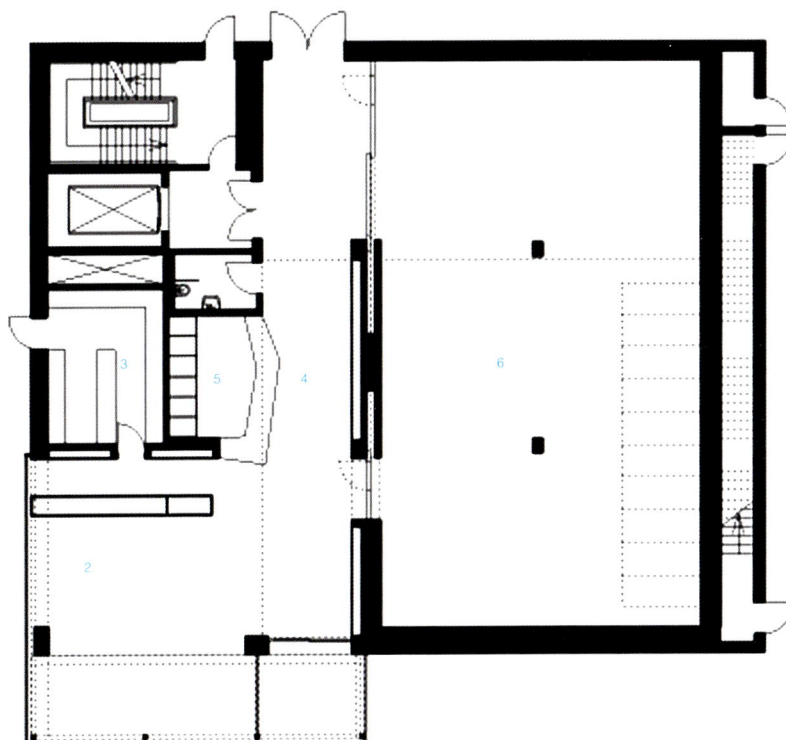

1. Ground floor foyer and reception leading into the café with site specific ceiling installation by Hew Locke
2. View of main gallery from mezzanine
3. First floor workshop studio

Prism Contemporary Art/Plastic Sensations

Location: West Hollywood, USA **Designed by:** PATTERNS **Completion dates:** 2009 **Photos©:** Joshua White **Area:** 700 sqm

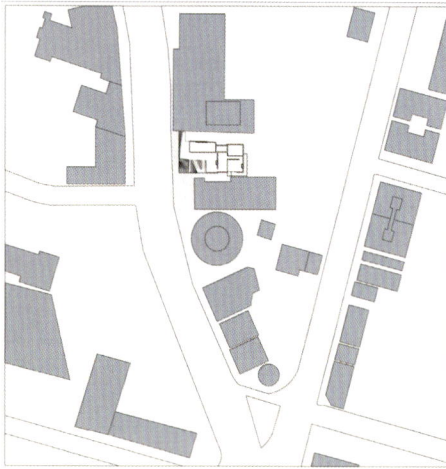

The project's legal status as a renovation of an existing structure placed unique restrictions upon the scope of work and the inflections within the façade's surface. An existing steel column grid left from a previous renovation predetermined floor-to-floor heights, and areas of existing stucco exterior walls from the original building provided opportunities for playful exchanges and guided the development of the design.

The gallery envelope is designed to create subtle sensations by inducing a physical and optical dynamism that both challenges and enhances the pedestrian movement along the iconic Sunset Strip. Its formal logic is the outcome of a productive negotiation between the ordering structural grid of the existing building and the intense vitality of the context.

Almost theatrically, the façade surfaces appear to lift up and then down, dramatically opening the interior while suspending its mass over the strip and projecting a sense of weightiness for pedestrian and vehicular traffic approaching from the west. Deeply inspired by the supple forms, streamlined detailing and plastic finishes of automotive design, the façade has a dual aesthetic performance associated with plastic materiality and responsive to its lively context: it behaves as a reflectively glossy surface during the day and as a viscously translucent skin when lit from inside at night.

As part of the collaboration with 3Form, a series of full-scale prototypes was developed and fabricated as an essential part of the design process. These prototypes were used to test various conditions affecting performance and aesthetics, cost and construction: from the limits of structure and its connections to mullions and polycarbonate panels, to issues pertaining to waterproofing and the behaviour of a glossy translucent surface, to the examination of custom assembly details and connections that support and seal the finished façade.

The material solution for the façade involves resin-based polycarbonate panels, which are colour dyed and extruded in a single pull. Colour and translucence are entirely design controlled. Panels were heat-formed over medium-density fiberboard (MDF) molds. All waterproofing and thermal expansion and contraction are taken up by hardware at the face of the panels, freeing the façade from any substrate or interior wall.

1. View from street
2. Front view from the Sunset Boulevard
3. View from the Sunset Boulevard at dusk

1

2

1, 2. Interior view from the first level towards the upper helix
3. Interior view towards staircase
4. Interior view at the first level towards terrace access

3

4

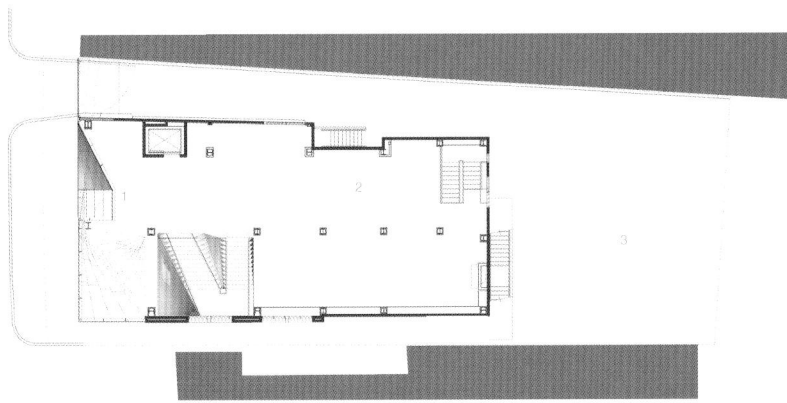

Ground floor plan
1. Main entrance
2. Gallery space
3. Parking

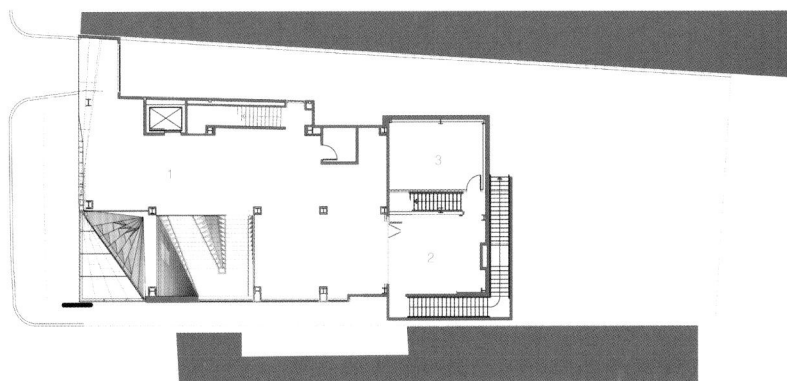

First floor plan
1. Gallery space
2. Private gallery space
3. Office

The Brother Stephen Debourg Performing Arts Centre

Location: South Australia, Australia **Designed by:** Tridente Architects **Completion date:** 2008 **Photos©:** Peter Fisher **Area:** 1,420 sqm

As the first major project to be implemented after master planning the entire senior school campus, the Brother Stephen Debourg Performing Arts Centre at Sacred Heart College demonstrates the schools' focus and a return to its core philosophy of being a teaching institution of its time, maintaining the provision of services par excellence.

Reinforcing the fledgling performing arts stream, the new facility signifies this change by the intervention of a contemporary building into a historically significant precinct and prominent location on the grounds. Bridging between existing traditional building stock, the performing art facility nestles comfortably within a grove of established trees in the manicured landscape. The splayed wings of the building offered to the driveway drawing one to the glazed entry and within.

The use of a coloured panelling system in cardinal purple offers more than just a tenuous link to the adjacent chapel; imbuing the internal spaces and the cloister with a subtle lilac glow to reinforce the spiritual and reverential ambience.

With a programme more complex and variable than the simple forms belie, the facility comfortably blends teaching and performance with other ancillary functions enabling it to be utilised by the college, feeder schools and affiliated colleges in the local area.

The use of construction techniques and materials more commonly associated with warehouses has minimised the cost of the base building allowing emphasis to be placed on the internal spaces and facilities. Integration and concealment of services was critical to accommodate the high level of acoustic control and isolation required of the teaching, practice and performance spaces and the quality expected of publicly accessible spaces.

Where possibility of use of day lighting has been maximised by the provision of large expanses of glazing, predominately orientated to the south. Elsewhere compact fluorescent and T5 fluorescent fittings have been utilised. With the specific acoustic requirements for performances, practice and studio work it was not possible to utilise any forms of passive ventilation and a reverse cycle air conditioning system has been adopted throughout, with windows generally sealed. To control running costs and reduce energy consumption an economy cycle system has been implemented to utilise unconditioned external air.

1. Entrance yard and access to the entrance
2. Façade view from lawn
3. Side view

1. Hallway and staircase
2. Performing arts centre

1. Display
2. Store
3. Observation
4. Foyer
5. Performing arts
6. Drama
7. Greenroom
8. Accessible toilet
9. Cloister
10. Male toilet
11. Female toilet
12. Plant room
13. Music room
14. Corridor
15. Kitchen
16. Reception
17. Studio
18. General music room
19. Control platform

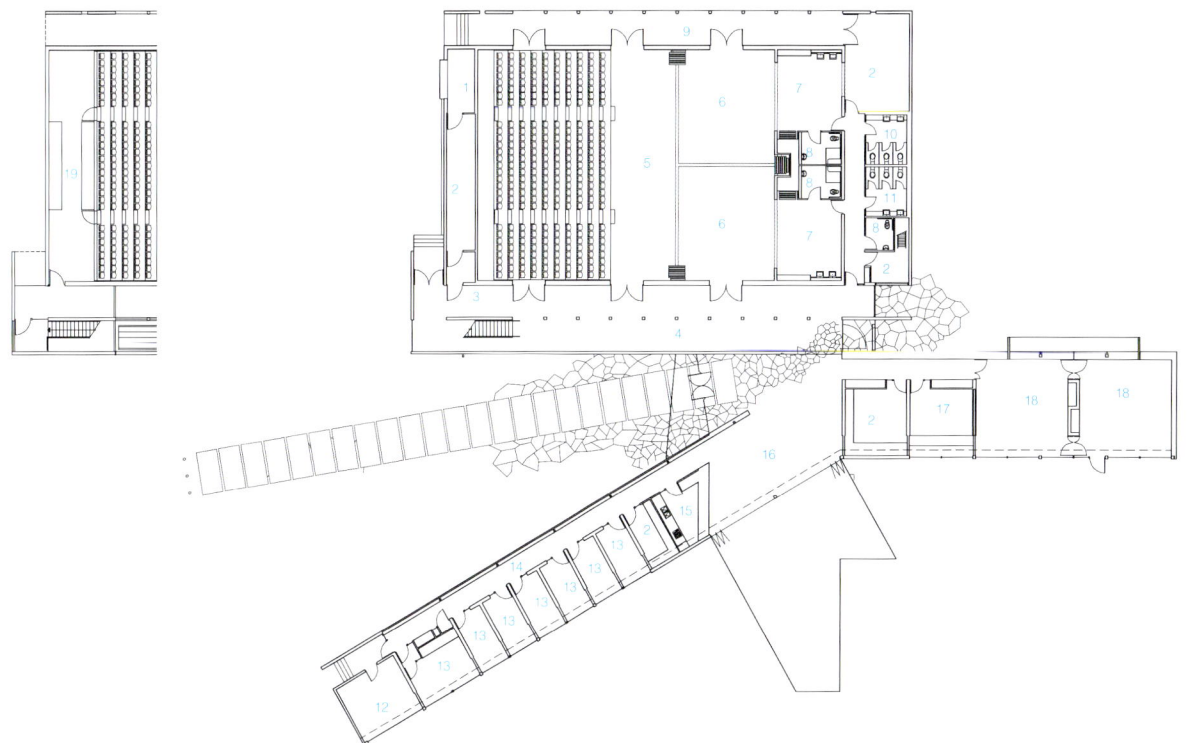

Location: Hämeenlinna, Finland **Designed by:** JKMM Architects **Completion date:** 2007 **Photos©:** Arno de la Chapelle, Jussi Tiainen, Patric Rastenberger **Awards:** Glass Structure Award 2008; The Forum AID Award, Best Nordic Interior Design 2007, Nominee; Steel Structure Award 2007

Verkatehdas Arts and Congress Centre

Verkatehdas consists of a 30,000 square metres early 20th century fabric factory complex, which is now redeveloped into a cultural institution in Hämeenlinna locating in southern Finland. New annexes are called Verkatehdas Arts & Congress Centre, adding up to a one-third of the whole. The complexity of the final compositions intriguing structure could be compared with a medieval city. Project places a new concert hall within the existing factory courtyard. New annex with movie theatres will be efficiently visible in the townscape. A large glazed inner courtyard forms the primary space and functional heart of the cultural factory. This fan-shaped courtyard opens up towards Vanajavesi water front park through foyer spaces.

The high gables of the old factory and new concert hall are dominating features in townscape. New structures respect old ones tuning the composition over again. The aim was to form a composition where the old mill complex, and new buildings form a harmonious entity, so that both together define the spirit of the place. Main materials are red brick, corten-steel, glass and concrete, and their handling is artless and plain. The new formal features and materials are kept in a simple and serene relationship with the old, thus emphasising the value of the existing structures like coarse surfaced concrete beams and brick masonry. Rough articulation of the whole enables to use strong colours and rustic surfaces like rubber, ceramics and rusted steel.

The concert hall is technologically sophisticated and transformable to allow multi-use of various performance types. The uses of concert hall vary from congresses to theatre performances, from classical music concerts with 700 seats, to rock concerts enabling 1,100 spectators. The cinema annex includes four movie theatres seating 650 all together. Movie theatres are equipped with modern digital techniques. In the future also large parts of the old factory will be renovated to house new functions, mainly educational and atelier spaces.

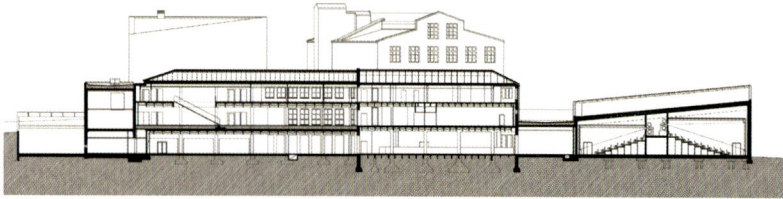

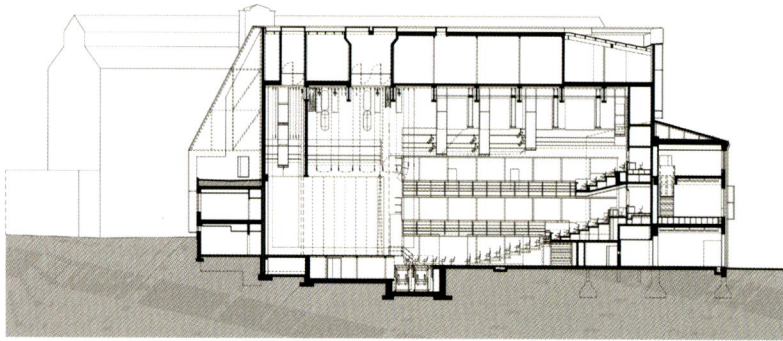

1. Entrance lobby
2. Outdoor café
3. Side view of entrance
4. Main entrance

3

4

1. Atrium
2. Box office

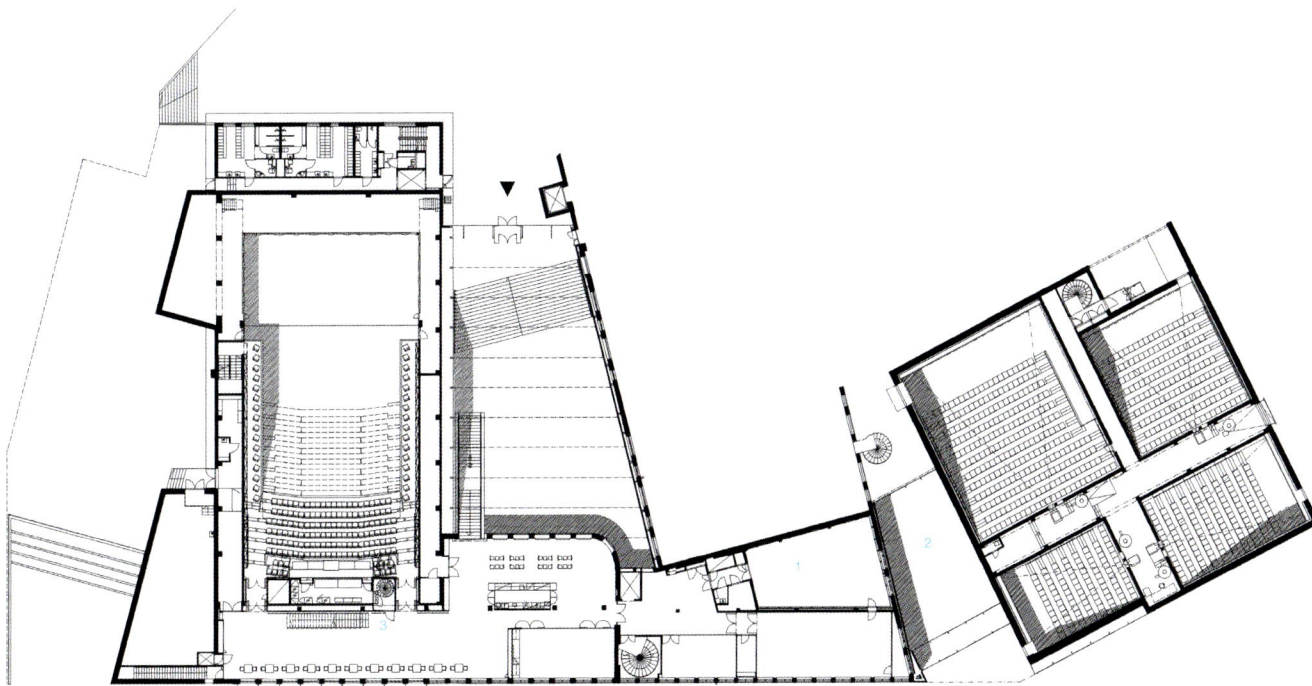

1. Conference rooms
2. Studio
3. Main foyer & bar

1 Restaurant
2, 3. Café
4. Stairs

3

4

1. Concert hall
2. Corridor
3. Concert hall stage

Peppermint Bay

Location: Hobart, Australia **Designed by:** TERROIR **Completion date:** 2005 **Photos©:** Brett Boardman
Site area: 1,000 sqm **Award:** 2007 Kenneth F. Brown Architecture Design Awards – Honourable Mention

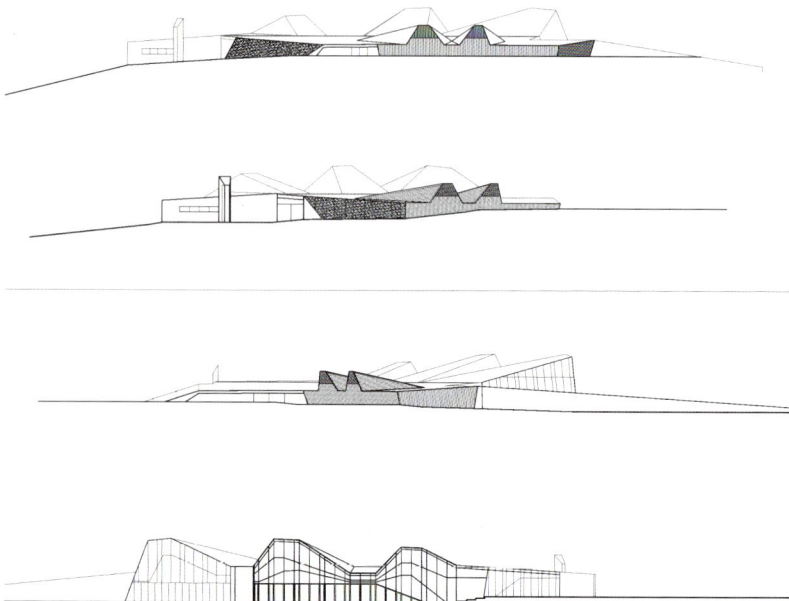

Peppermint Bay lies at the core of a multi-faceted tourism development, comprising a high speed multi-purpose cruise vessel from the Hobart waterfront or a 40-minute car journey through the D'Entrecasteaux Channel to a major waterside function and culinary venue at Peppermint Bay – an inlet on the River Derwent, located near the country town of Woodbridge, 40 kilometres south of Hobart. Peppermint Bay offers a presentation of the produce of the Channel region and Tasmania in general in a high-quality restaurant/function venue incorporating significant retail, boutique epicure food manufacture and a venue for art and craft makers from the region to retail their products.

The conception of the project is based around the picturesque journey to and from the peninsula, via river or road. This journey is integral to the visitor experience and generates a site response based in a continuation of this experience to the centre of the site. The destination itself is conceived not as a series of elements comprising building, garden, and associated features, but a singular, complex entity, the sum of which comprises a total "landscape" experience. Thus, the defining aspect and key image of the centre is in the reconfiguration of the peninsula into a single "garden" destination.

Peppermint Bay comprises public spaces divided into three zones, each of which has a precise and different relationship to the landscape. An intimate, "locals" bar hovers atop a small cliff to provide connection with the water below. The restaurant concentrates the view across the bay to the horizon while the function area gathers itself opposite the oak tree at the termination of the labyrinthine route.

The client desired an iconic building from minimal expenditure, therefore Peppermint Bay was constructed from familiar materials (such as the steel frame and metal cladding) that permitted architectural significance in their arrangement and detailing. The minimisation of the materials palette allowed an increase in the potential to highly resolve and finish such familiar materials. For instance, the roof cladding is an example of a commonplace material pushed to its maximum effect.

1. Back façade
2. Façade detail
3. The entrance

PEPPERMINT
BAY

1. View from the back façade
2. Side view
3. The entrance

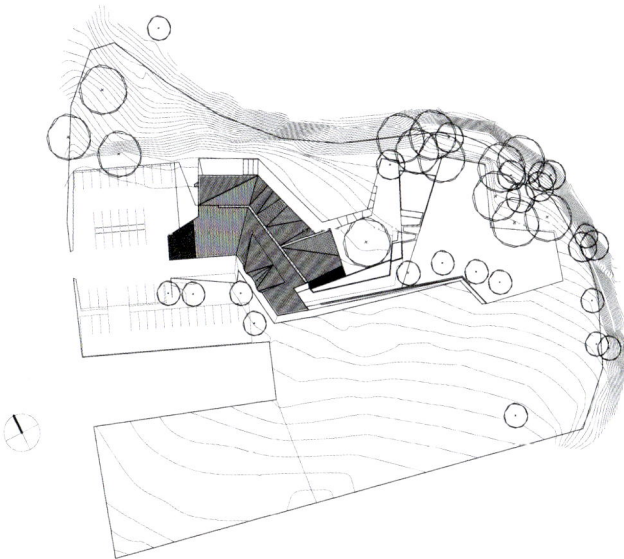

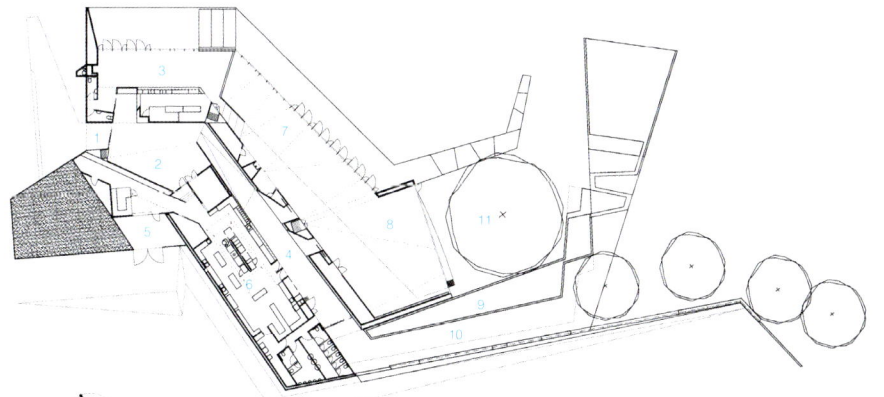

1. Entrance
2. Entrance hall
3. Bar
4. Walkway
5. Stores
6. Kitchen
7. Dining room
8. Function room
9. Fish race
10. Herb wall
11. Oak tree

1, 2. The restaurant
3. Entrance of the restaurant

Art Gallery of Alberta

Location: Edmonton, Canada **Designed by:** Randall Stout Architects, Inc. **Completion date:** 2009
Photos©: Robert Lemermeyer

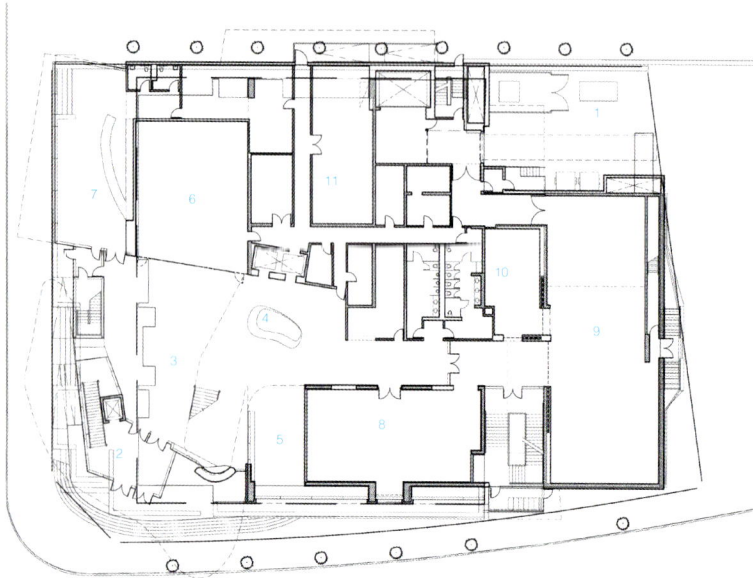

The new Art Gallery of Alberta is an engaging and inviting visual arts centre in downtown Edmonton, Alberta. Celebrating its prominent location on Sir Winston Churchill Square, the city's arts and government core, the building's architectural design formally and philosophically extends out into the community, welcoming visitors of all ages and backgrounds to experience contemporary art firsthand. Designed by Los Angels-based Randall Stout Architects, the Gallery opened to the public in January 2010.

Crafted of patinaed zinc, high performance glazing, and stainless steel, the building has a timeless appearance and extraordinary durability in the northern climate. Transparent glazing planes and reflective metal surfaces animate the building, exposing the activities within and engaging people and art at multiple levels on both the interior and exterior.

Selected to reflect Edmonton's dramatic weather patterns and the extreme contrast of the long days of summer and the short days of winter, these materials create a dynamic quality that allow the building to transform along with its natural surroundings. Not only does the building change throughout the day, it changes from season to season. More static building materials would not allow for this type of ephemeral connection between the building and the site.

The design reinvents the museum's public spaces through a continuous stainless steel surface that moves lithely through the museum's interior and exterior spaces. Wall and ceiling become one fluid surface, which captures the spatial volume while guiding the public through entrance points, wrapping event and gathering spaces, and leading on to the galleries.

Galleries were conceived as more conventional spaces in order to maximise flexibility for curators and maintain the high level of environmental control necessary to house travelling exhibitions and the Gallery's collection. On the exterior, the galleries are expressed as simple stacked rectangular boxes, establishing a dialogue with the existing building mass as well as a heightened juxtaposition with the undulating surfaces of the public spaces. These two languages of mass and curvilinear form define an inviting rhythm of destination and path in a unique way-finding experience for visitors.

1. Art handling/storage
2. Main entrance vestibule
3. Main lobby
4. Reception desk
5. Gift shop
6. Gallery great hall
7. Gallery café
8. Special collection gallery
9. Ernest J. Poole gallery
10. Children's gallery
11. Catering kitchen

1. The entrance
2. Façade detail
3. Dusk view

1. Lobby and lounge area
2. Entrance lobby

1. Gallery
2. Dining hall

2

De Hangar, Eindhoven

Location: Eindhoven, The Netherlands **Designed by:** diederendirrix b.v. **Completion date:** 2009 **Photos©:** Arthur Bagen **Construction area:** 8,600 sqm **Award:** Dirk Roosenburgprijs 2009 (Biennial Eindhoven Architecture Prize)

1. Elementary school
2. Day care centre
3. Infant care
4. Children's library
5. Community centre
6. Sports centre
7. Youth centre
8. Covered area (square)

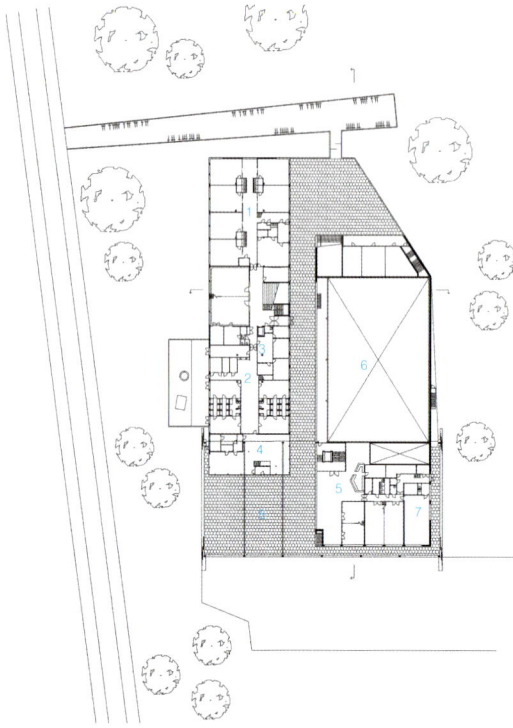

In the centre of Meerhoven, a Vinex-district in Eindhoven, lies a characteristic airplane hanger, together with several other important industrial inheritances, it keeps the memory of the former airfield Welschap alive. With the redevelopment and expansion into a complex for education and recreation, the hanger is transformed into a vital cultural centre for the district. To house the extensive programme two volumes were added, which were slidden into the building. A large part of the hanger has been kept empty, which allows space for a covered square, that also functions as the entrance to the complex. A central corridor, also covered by the hanger, connects the square to a public playground that opens towards the planned ecological green zone. The corridor is enclosed on one side by a colourful, transparent volume that houses a community centre with library. On the other side lies a volume situated partially in the ground, with a playground on the roof. It houses a sports centre and a gathering space. The buildings are connected by way of an underground volume that contains the changing rooms for the gym.

1. Overall view of the building
2. Part of façade viewed from the lawn
3. Inner courtyard

1. Exercising hall
2. Interior hallway and outer play yard are divided by glass wall
3. Foyer and stairs

3

Cultuurfabriek

Location: Veenendaal, The Netherlands **Designed by:** Jos van Eldonk **Completion date:** 2010 **Photos©:** Daria Scagliola; Stijn Brakkee/Raoul Suermondt **Construction area:** 4,700 sqm

In the new city centre of Veenendaal, the former Hollandia wool factory is being converted into a culture cluster, housing the library, the Het Kleine Veenlo Museum, the historical society and the art-lending facility. The design was approached first from an urban design perspective. Because the complex is not located along the main route, it has been linked to a new building. This new building ensures that the main entrance is located on the new Kees Stipplein and connects to the new street structure. The old factory chimney was retained, in the courtyard between the old building and the new edifice. Because the tower is now somewhat hidden, it mainly works at a distance, in the Veenendaal skyline, and you only see it again once you are inside the culture cluster.

The Nervi-like columns in the new building that end in the support structure for the floors are inspired by the industrial concrete structure of the old factory. This stacking of columns and floors has been made visible from the square through the glass façade. The knitting patterns incorporated in the outer walls refer to Veenendaal's wool tradition. As in knitting, the brick walls feature variations in colour and relief, creating light and dark effects. They are brick Scandinavian jumpers in cable stitch and moss stitch, as it were, with a trim underneath that serves as a classical plinth. Weaving patterns can also be found in the play of flat and moulded click-bands in the façade.

1. Old factory chimney © Raoul Suermondt
2. South façade © Daria Scagliola and Stijn Brakkee
3. Fronts to square © Daria Scagliola and Stijn Brakkeel
4. New and old façades © Daria Scagliola and Stijn Brakkee

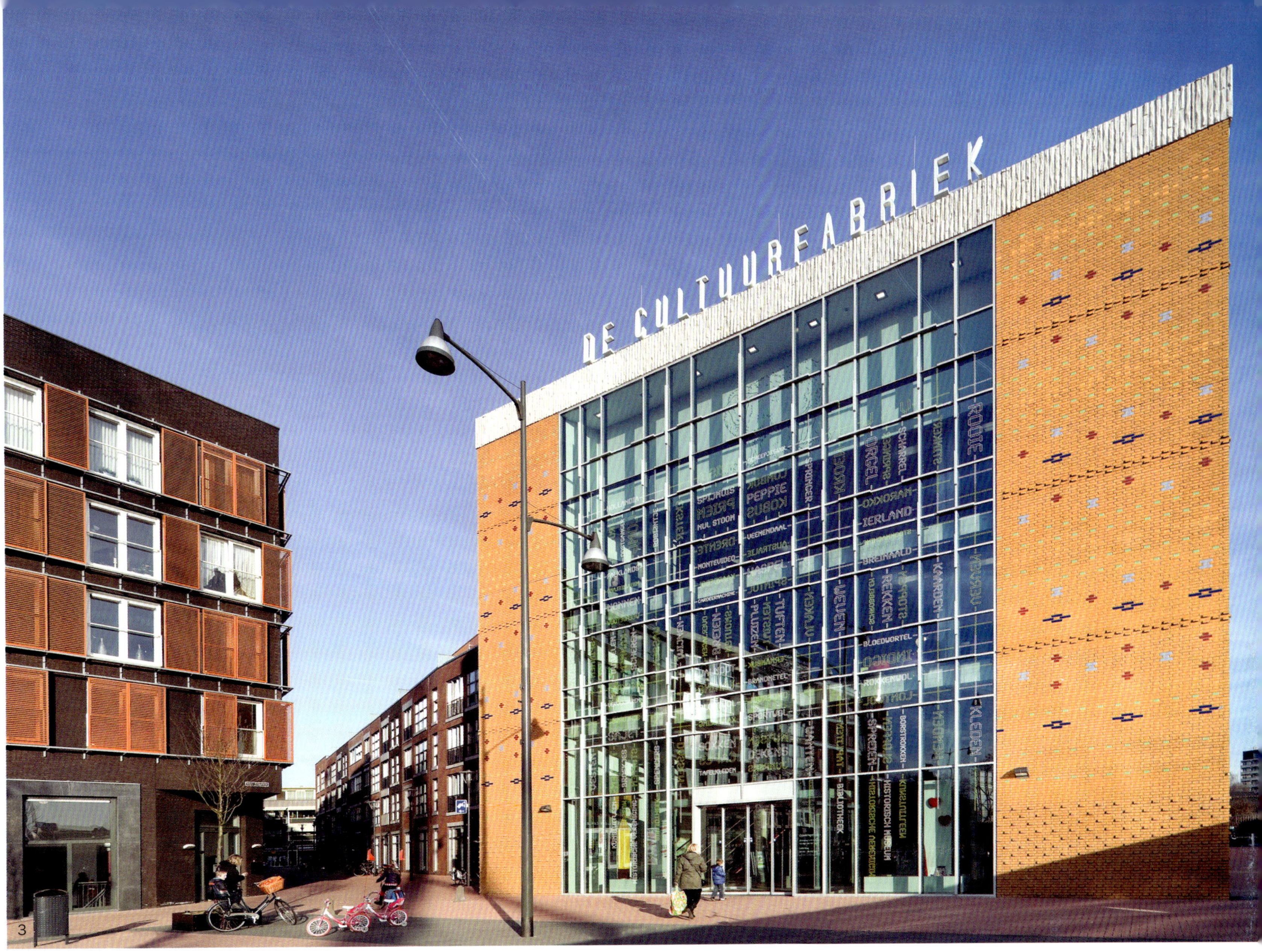

3

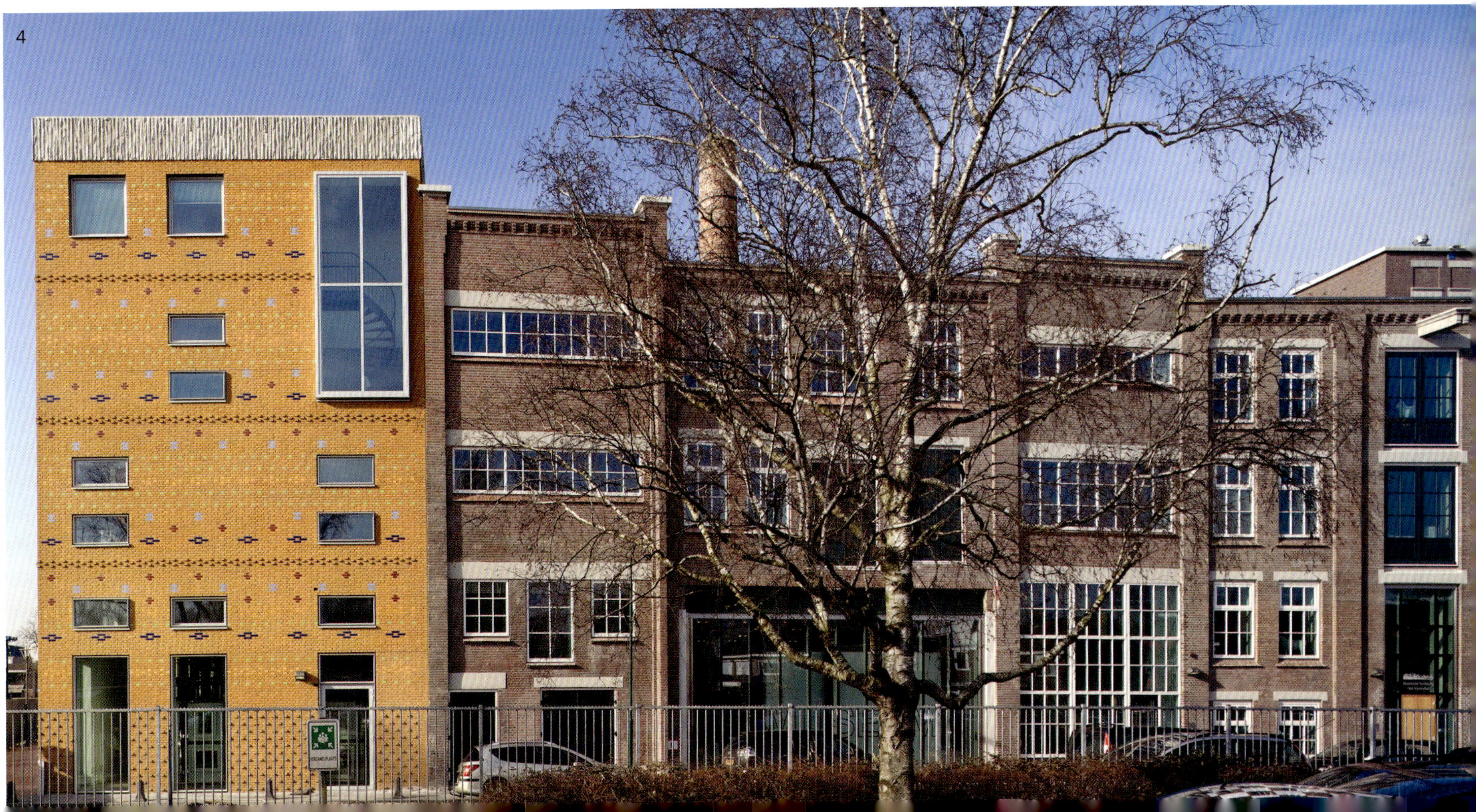

4

1. Library © Daria Scagliola and Stijn Brakkee
2. Coffee shop on the ground floor © Raoul Suermondt
3. Entrance hall © Daria Scagliola and Stijn Brakkeel

3

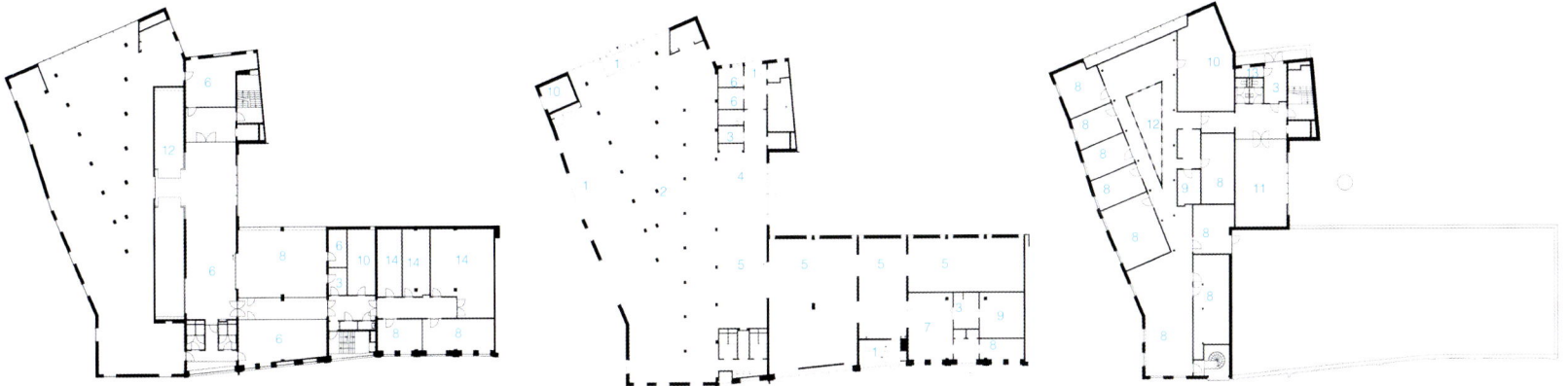

1. Entrance
2. Art library
3. Kitchen
4. Café
5. Museum
6. Library
7. Conference room
8. Office
9. Archives
10. Technical space
11. Canteen
12. Void
13. Outdoor
14. Storage

Messel Pit Visitor Information Centre

Location: Messel, Germany **Designed by:** landau + kindelbacher architekten **Completion date:** 2010 **Photos©:** landau + kindelbacher / Jan Bitter **Construction area:** 2,060 square metres **Awards:** Representative Buildings in state of Hessen, special recognition, 2011; Nominated for Mies Arch, European Union Prize 2011

The task of designing a visitor information centre for the Messel fossil pit, listed as a UNESCO World Natural Heritage site, demanded intense consideration of the turbulent history of the place, of both the scientific origin and the changing history of the site itself.

The chronological room sequence guides visitors intuitively through the exhibition, allowing them to succumb to their attractions undisturbed. Following the orientation in the generously sized foyer, the round tour begins with a visit to the cinema – a place of arrival and unwinding in which an introductory film offers an overview of the site and its changing history.

Starting with the room dedicated to portraying the origin of a maar lake, the exhibition continues as a recurring theme through all the rooms: with a leap in time to the period 47 million years ago, the visitor symbolically enters the interior of the Earth. In a virtual plunge, the visitor dives down to 433 metres below the ground level – assisted by acoustic and visual simulations. On firm ground again, one physically walks through selected parts of the real research core. Starting at the Earth's core, one progresses "upwards" in the dark narrow mine-like room towards the light. There one can visit the adjoining theme gardens arranged in a flowing transition, or continue inside with the round tour. In contrast to the constricted core, a high, light-flooded room now opens up to the visitor, intended to convey the atmosphere of a rain forest. Life in and around the former Messel lake becomes visible and tangible through the use of elements of today's jungles and lakes.

In the next room, a model laboratory is used to demonstrate the different stages and methods of a preparation that enables the fossil treasures to be extracted durably from the sensitive material that is oil shale. The highlight and at the same time the conclusion of the exhibition is the treasure chamber, where partly alternating preparations are artistically and attractively presented. This room appears like a jewel casket.

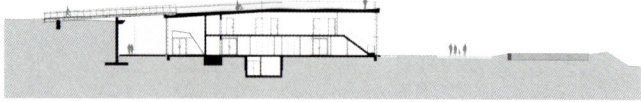

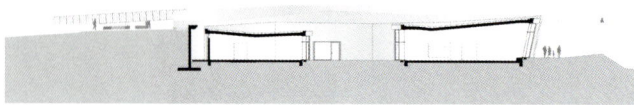

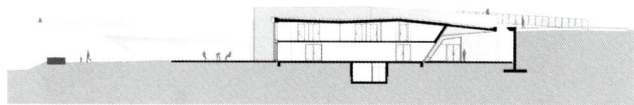

1, 2. Front view
3. Entrance

1, 2. Foyer
3. Lower foyer viewed from the upper level

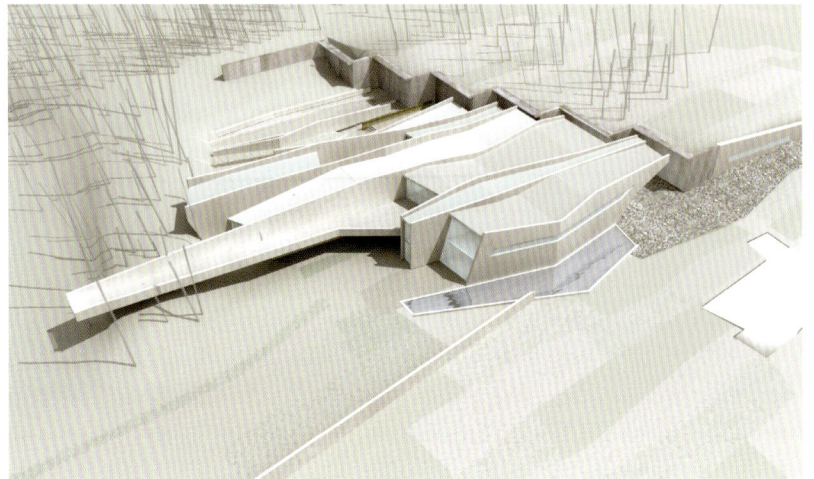

3

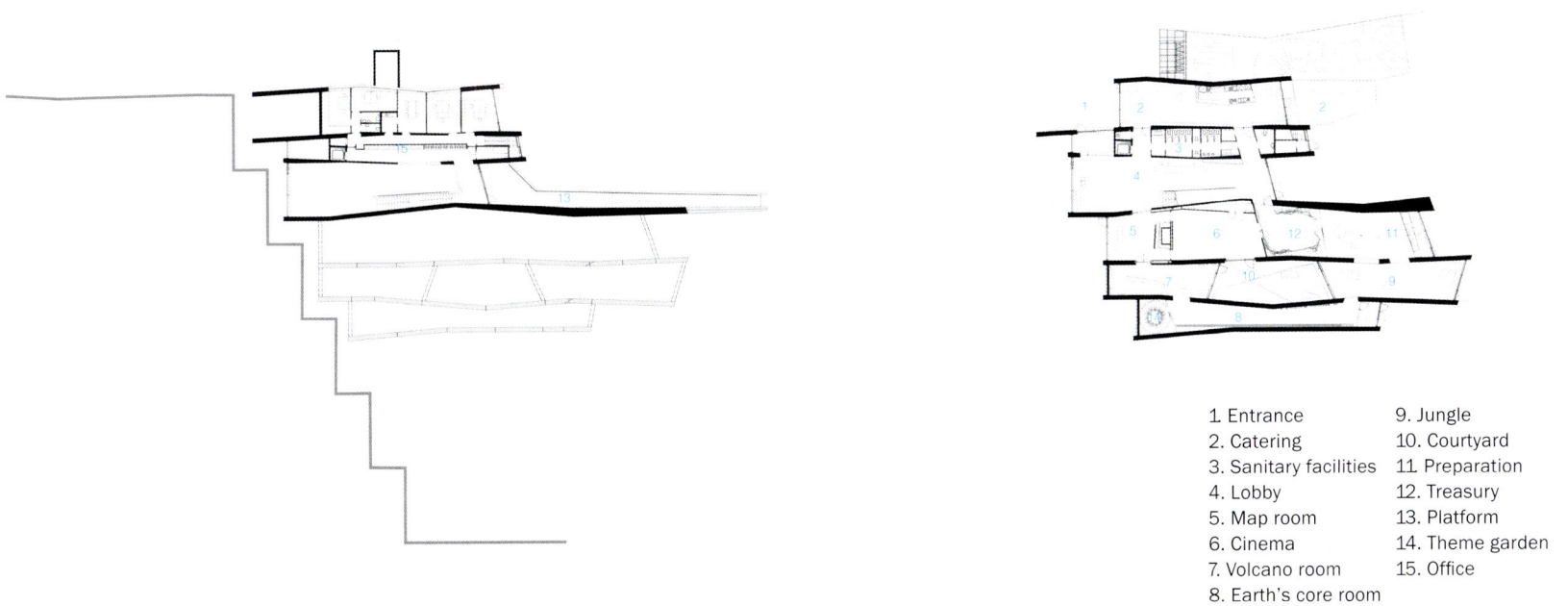

1. Entrance
2. Catering
3. Sanitary facilities
4. Lobby
5. Map room
6. Cinema
7. Volcano room
8. Earth's core room
9. Jungle
10. Courtyard
11. Preparation
12. Treasury
13. Platform
14. Theme garden
15. Office

1. Exhibition room - earth's core
2. Exhibition detail
3, 4. Exhibition room – volcano

1 Exhibition room - jungle
2, 3. Exhibition room – preparation
4. Exhibition room - earth's core

3

4

Provintial Mediatheque Ugo Casiraghi

Location: Gorizia, Italy **Designed by:** waltritsch a+u / Arch. Dimitri Waltritsch **Completion date:** 2011 **Photos©:** Marco Covi **Area:** 500 square metres

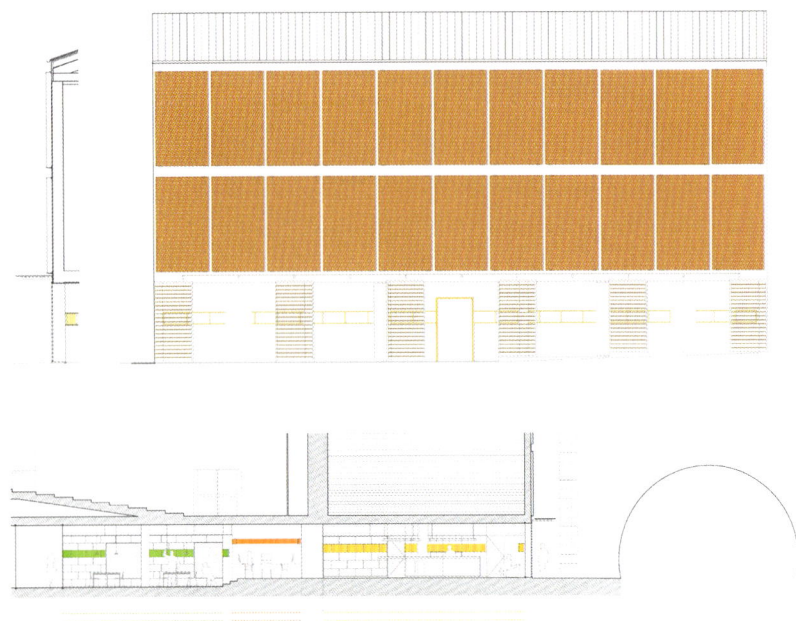

The new Mediatheque is part of a larger complex named Casa del Cinema – Home of the Film, which includes the Kinemax multiplex, several associations dedicated to the cinema culture, the DAMS Cinema section of the Udine University, and finally the Mediatheque. One place, located between the city main square and the castle hill, which gathers commercial, cultural, educational and promotional activities dedicated to the film culture. This combination of different activities is obviously quite unique, and particularly important for the small city of Gorizia. The Mediatheque stands on the ground floor between the street and one internal passage, so it has two entrances, facing the city as well as the University.

The simple plan layout divides the space into three main areas open to the public: the newspaper and magazines hall, the study space and the video room. Behind the reception and reference point, which is visually connected to both entrances, the are separated rooms as storage and one office. All spaces are bound by book and media shelves at full height. One shelve line is marked by a strong colour, different for every area, providing specific identity. The same coloured shelve line defines the glass façades as well, becoming a communication vitrine, where visitors directly expose new arrivals, or organise a small exhibition directly facing the public street. The newspaper and magazine area have a custom-designed star-shape reading table and a cross shape information counter, and is thought for informal gathering. The tables in the study room can be reorganised in order to host reading evenings or presentations.

Part of the project is the new façade on the public street as well. A series of coloured glass panels on the higher part of the façade are facing the built and natural context of the historical city heart. The dialogue with the surrounding buildings goes through the use of the typical colour palette of the building render, and the slight and not intrusive reflection of the surroundings provided by the coloured glass. This allows the context to be dilated into the Mediatheque building façade: a "form of transit" of the everyday life.

1,3. Side view of the building
2. Front view

1

2

1. Entrance of library
2. View of library through glass wall
3. Interior of library

3

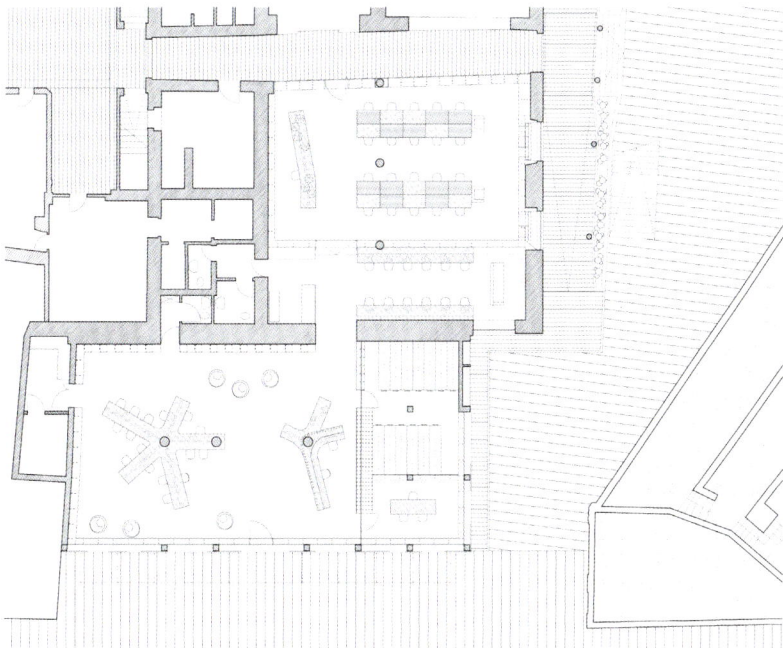

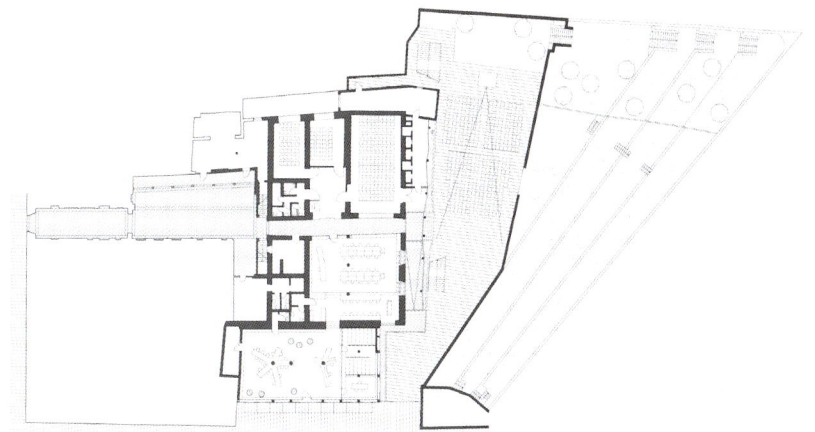

1

2

1-4. Interior of information room / reading area

Cool Art and Culture Centre

Location: Heerhugowaard, The Netherlands **Designed by:** Jos van Eldonk **Completion date:** 2008
Photos©: Daria Scagliola, Stijn Brakkee/Raoul Suermondt **Site area:** 4,780 square metres

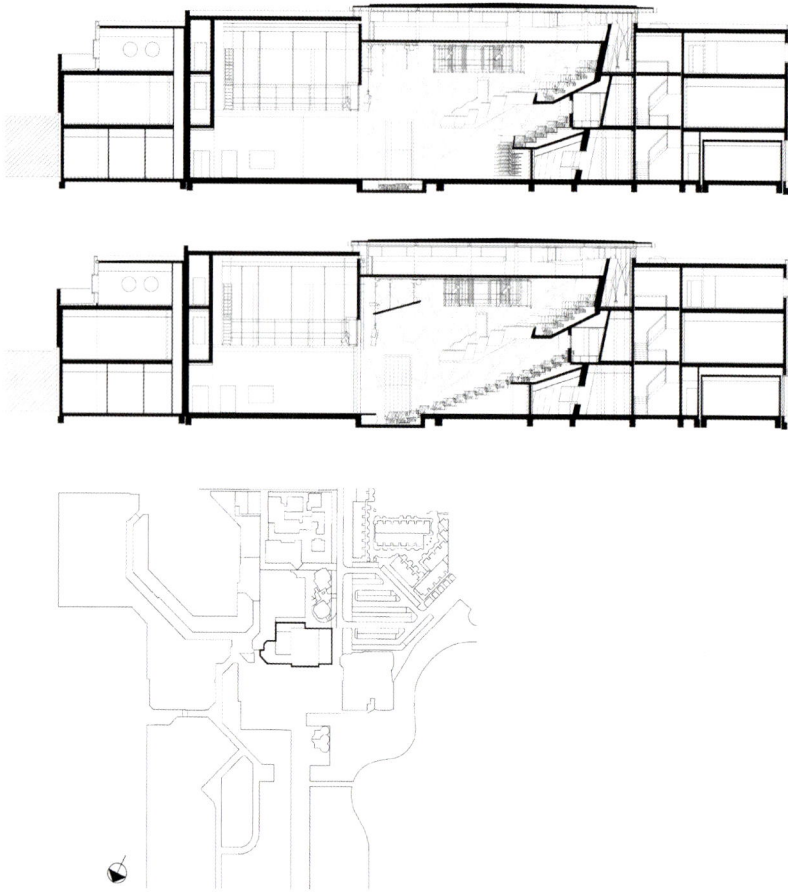

The Cool Art and Culture Centre in Heerhugowaard is the fusion of a theatre, a music school, a creativity centre and a café-restaurant. The building stands on a prominent spot in the new city centre of Heerhugowaard, at the top of a new boulevard. The new city hall and the library are located at the other end of this axis. The dominant shape of the theatre is strictly rectangular, conforming to the orthogonal urban design of the new city centre.

The brief called for creating a building that was dramatic and yet contextual, but there were no characteristic themes to be found in the vicinity that could be used to give the building an identity. The context consists of an anonymous, inward-directed shopping centre in grey concrete. Neither did Heerhugowaard's history provide many inspiring clues. Ultimately the context became literal and associative: the Heerhugowaard coat of arms and the red cabbage cultivated in this area. They provided motifs to give the building an identity.

The heart of the building – the theatre auditorium – is the abstraction of a red cabbage. The stairs to the auditorium are situated between the "leaves" of this cabbage. On the outside of the building, one can recognise the Heerhugowaard coat of arms: two herons on either side of ears of wheat. The abstracted, grey-hued feather pattern of the herons is visible in the façade, made of glazed tiles. The ears of wheat are represented by the yellow and green pillars at the main entrance in the centre of the building. The pillars branch out toward the top into blades with glittering lights at the tips. The column theme continues inside, where columns support the roof of the foyer. The main auditorium is a combination of a classical hemispherical theatre and a black-box theatre: the seats can be shifted and the stage can be lowered.

1. Front view in the dusk
2. Façade detail
3. Entrance detail

1. Side view of overall building
2. Overall building viewed from the parking zone
3. Reception / information desk
4. Stairs

3

4

1. Foyer
2. Booking office/reception
3. Dressing room
4. Kitchen
5. Office
6. Greenroom
7. Elevator
8. Storeroom
9. Technical space
10. Theatre
11. Stage
12. Cloakroom
13. Toilet
14. Music education
15. Café
16. Canteen
17. Terrace
18. Expedition
19. Direction room
20. Studio
21. Entrance

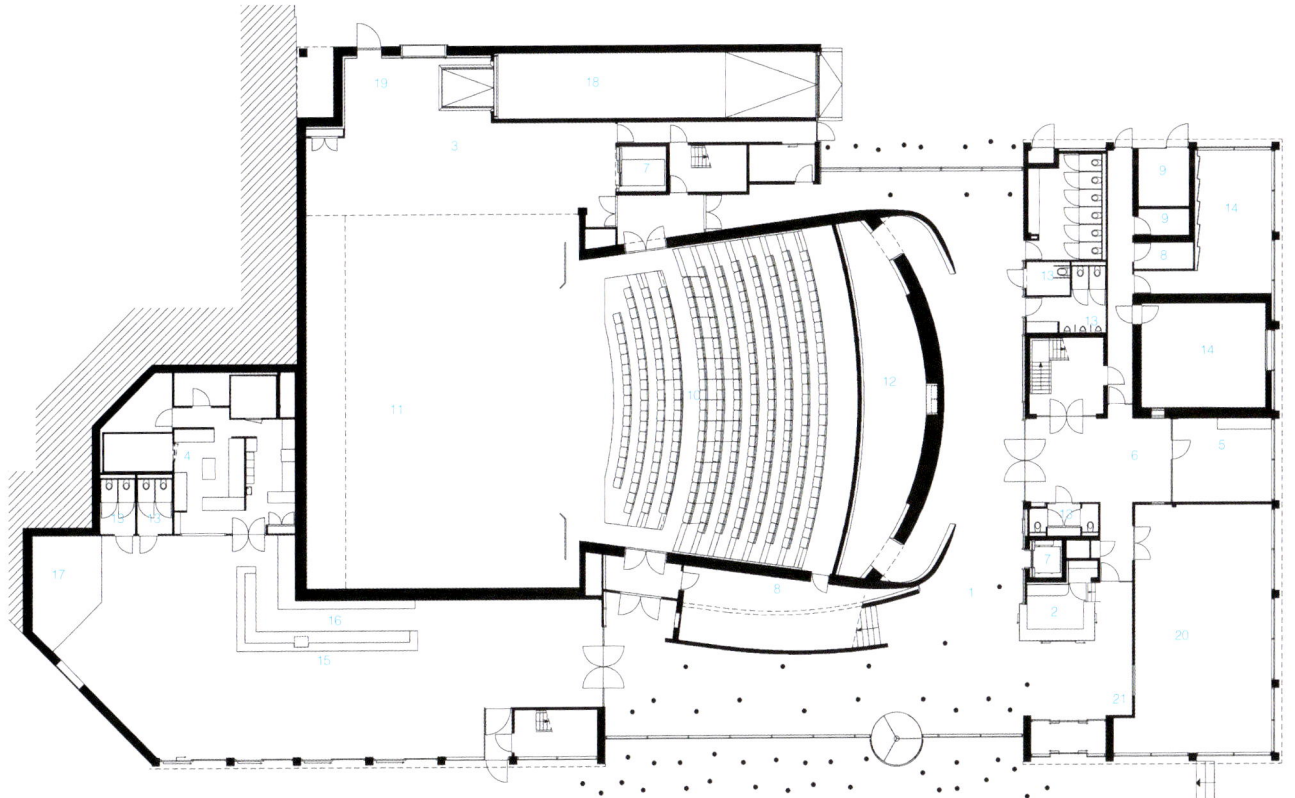

1 Café / bar
2. Dance room
3. Auditorium
4. Auditorium detail

Index

A
ACXT Architects
www.acxt.net

Alvaro Planchuelo
www.alvaroplanchuelo.com

Architects Lahdelma & Mahlamäki
www.ark-l-m.fi

architekturbüro HALLE 1
www.halle1.at

Armon Choros architektonikis
www.armon-architects.com

Arquitectonica
www.arquitectonica.com

B
Brière, Gilbert + Associés, Architecture & Design Urbain
www.brieregilbert.com

D
DAP studio
http://dapstudio.com

diederendirrix b.v.
www.diederendirrix.nl

F
Fuksas
www.fuksas.it

FÜNDC (C. GARCIA & P. MARTIN, Architects)
http://fundc.com

G
gmp – von Gerkan, Marg and Partners Architects
www.gmp-architekten.de

Gudmundur Jonsson Arkitektkontor
www.gudmundurjonsson.no

H
Heriberto Hernández Ochoa, Raúl Juárez Perezlete, Jorge Hernández Luquín
www.leap.mx

Hoz Fontan Arquitectos
www.hozfontanarquitectos.com

I
inFORM Studio
http://in-formstudio.com

J
JAKOB+MACFARLANE
www.jakobmacfarlane.com

JDS Architects
http://jdsarchitects.com

JKMM Architects
www.jkmm.fi

J. MAYER H.
www.jmayerh.de

Jos van Eldonk
www.soetersvaneldonk.nl

Juan Navarro Baldeweg
www.navarrobaldeweg.net

K

KSP Jürgen Engel Architekten
www.ksp-architekten.de

L

LAN Architecture
www.lan-paris.com

landau + kindelbacher architekten
www.landaukindelbacher.de

Lateral Arquitectura & Diseño
www.lateral.cl

M

MacGabhann Architects
www.macgabhannarchitects.ie

Max Dudler
www.maxdudler.de

Menkès Shooner Dagenais LeTourneux Architectes
http://msdl.ca

P

PATTERNS
www.p-a-t-t-e-r-n-s.net

Philip Weddle/ Weddle Gilmore
http://weddlegilmore.com

Preston Scott Cohen
http://pscohen.com

Promontorio Architects
www.promontorio.net

R

Randall Stout Architects, Inc.
www.stoutarc.com

Ricardo Bofill Taller de Arquitectura
www.bofill.com

RMDM Architects
www.rmdm.fr

RTKL
www.rtkl.com

S

Søren Robert Lund Arkitekter and Studio NORD
www.srlarkitekter.dk

Stanley Saitowitz/Natoma Architects
www.saitowitz.com

Studio Macola
www.studiomacola.it

T

TEK Architects
www.tek-arch.com

TERROIR
www.terroir.com.au

Treusch Architecture
www.treusch.at

Tridente Architects
www.tridente.com.au

W

waltritsch a+u
www.wapu.it

©2010 by Design Media Publishing Limited
This edition published in June 2012

Design Media Publishing Limited
20/F Manulife Tower
169 Electric Rd, North Point
Hong Kong
Tel: 00852-28672587
Fax: 00852-25050411
E-mail: Kevinchoy@designmediahk.com
www.designmediahk.com

Editing: YIN Qian
Proofreading: YIN Qian
Design/Layout: ZHAO Cong

ISBN 978-988-15450-5-3

Printed in China